Mastering the Art of
Commercial Real Estate Investing

MASTERING
the Art of
COMMERCIAL
REAL ESTATE
INVESTING

How to Successfully Build Wealth & Grow Passive
Income from Your Rental Properties

DOUG MARSHALL, CCIM

NEW YORK
LONDON • NASHVILLE • MELBOURNE • VANCOUVER

Mastering the Art of Commercial Real Estate Investing

How to Successfully Build Wealth and Grow Passive Income from Your Rental Properties

Published in New York, New York, by Morgan James Publishing. Morgan James is a trademark of Morgan James, LLC. www.MorganJamesPublishing.com

ISBN 9781642790153 paperback
ISBN 9781642790160 eBook
Library of Congress Control Number: 2018936396

Cover Design by:
Mia Broder Designs

Interior Design by:
Chris Treccani
www.3dogcreative.net

Morgan James is a proud partner of Habitat for Humanity Peninsula and Greater Williamsburg. Partners in building since 2006.

Get involved today! Visit
MorganJamesPublishing.com/giving-back

To all the real estate investors I've met through the years who have struggled with building wealth and growing passive income from their rental properties. This book is for you.

What Is a CCIM?

In 1999, Doug Marshall received the prestigious CCIM designation, which many consider the PhD of commercial real estate. A Certified Commercial Investment Member (CCIM) is a recognized expert in the disciplines of commercial and investment real estate. The designation is awarded by the CCIM Institute. Today almost 70 percent of designees hold the title of owner, partner, principal, or president, representing an exclusive worldwide referral network of thirteen thousand members in thirty countries. CCIMs must be proficient in the areas of investment analysis, market analysis, user decision analysis, and financial analysis for commercial real estate. Of the more than 150,000 commercial real estate professionals in the United States, only an estimated 7 percent hold the CCIM designation.[1]

Contents

How to Achieve Financial Freedom

How do you become good at something?
Firstly, learn how it is done. Secondly, learn how others do it.
Then do it your own way.
–Kyos Magupe, philosopher

Do you want to supplement your current income by investing in commercial real estate (CRE)? Better yet, would you like to someday quit your day job and devote your energies exclusively to your rental properties? If that's your plan, then this book is for you. This book is for the commercial real estate investor who is either new to investing or has been at it for a while but realizes he or she needs help learning the time-proven principles of real estate investing.

With more than thirty-five years of experience financing real estate, including a decade of personally investing in rental properties, I have learned how to successfully invest in commercial real estate, sometimes unfortunately by doing it the hard way. My clients and I have learned the do's and don'ts of CRE investing, but there is no reason you have to go through the same learning process of trial and error. By sharing my knowledge with you, the hope is that you can avoid the pitfalls I've made so you can grow your CRE investments more successfully and with significantly fewer setbacks along the way.

I have divided this book into four sections: buying, financing, managing, and selling investor-owned commercial real estate. Each section is filled with real-life examples and common sense advice on how to build wealth and grow passive income from your rental properties.

For example, in the *buying* section of the book, you'll learn:

- ➢ Why buying real estate is better than owning any other type of investment.
- ➢ What the real estate market cycle is, and what phase it is currently in.
- ➢ What the six immutable laws of real estate investing are.

In the *financing* section, I will explain, among other things:
- ➢ How you can get the best possible loan for your property.
- ➢ What six things you need to do to make your property lender friendly.
- ➢ What nine underwriting guidelines lenders use to qualify borrowers.

In the *managing* section, I will disclose:
- ➢ What the number one mistake most property owners make managing their apartments.
- ➢ What are the three most important things to consider when choosing a property management company.
- ➢ What seven hidden costs of managing apartments can cost you big-time.

And finally, in the *selling* section, you will discover:
- ➢ What five things you must do before you list your property for sale.
- ➢ Three traps on the purchase and sale agreement that the seller should negotiate away.
- ➢ What the benefits are of doing a 1031 Exchange.

As an investor myself, I have written *Mastering the Art of Commercial Real Estate Investing* for those investors needing assistance getting started. I believe this book will go a long way toward helping you take charge of your future. If you like easy-to-follow, solid advice and step-by-step instructions, you'll love this life-changing guide. You can bolster your income and begin the process of building wealth today!

THE BOOK'S TITLE

From my many years of commercial real estate experience, I've come to the realization that those who excel at CRE investing understand there is a lot more to it than crunching the numbers. Yes, you need to have a firm grasp on how to value real estate, how leveraging a property with debt will influence the property's return, and so on. But CRE investing is much more than that.

I've come to realize that the most successful real estate investors I've had the privilege to have as clients develop a subjective, intuitive feel about a property. They don't look at the potential acquisition as it is at the moment. Rather, they create a vision for the property. They envision what it would be like if it were renovated and managed correctly. They also realize how important it is to understand market trends, perceive how a neighborhood is trending, develop an awareness of where we are on the real estate market cycle … to name just a few factors worth knowing. These parameters are far more subjective than objective in scope. And that is why I titled my book *Mastering the Art of Commercial Real Estate Investing*. This type of investing is genuinely more of an art than a science.

Some may say that the subtitle, *How to Successfully Build Wealth and Grow Passive Income from Your Rental Properties*, is redundant—that building wealth and growing passive income are really the same thing. I beg to differ. Building wealth is all about increasing the investor's net worth over time. As an investor's CRE portfolio grows, so too should his or her net worth. Growing passive income, on the other hand, is all about maximizing cash flow after debt service. Whether passive income slowly grows over time depends a great deal on how a property is leveraged with debt. I've known investors who focused exclusively on building equity (increasing their net worth) to the detriment of generating cash flow. My CRE investing philosophy maintains that successful real estate investing should do both: it should build an investor's net worth, and it should grow his or her passive income.

KEY TERMS TO UNDERSTAND

To get started, you need to keep in mind some key terms. The following are my definitions, and they establish the way I use these terms in the book.

1. **Commercial Real Estate** – This is broadly defined as "property consisting of land and the buildings on it."[2] My definition has a much narrower scope: *Commercial real estate is any investor-owned, income-producing*

property. Based on my definition, commercial real estate includes single-family rental homes through multi-storied apartments as well as retail, office, industrial, hospitality, mobile home parks, and so on. On the other hand, my definition does *not* include:

➤ Your personal residence since your home does not generate cash flow.

➤ Undeveloped land as it does not generate cash flow.

➤ Owner-occupied properties because the owner is focused on the long-term profitability of his business, not on whether the real estate itself is generating good cash flow.

2. **Commercial Mortgage Broker** – This term is used in contrast to a residential mortgage broker. Residential mortgage brokers finance homes. They are unqualified to finance investor-owned properties. Commercial mortgage brokers, however, finance investor-owned, income-producing properties. This is an important distinction to keep in mind. So when I occasionally use the term *mortgage broker* in this book, I am referring to a commercial mortgage broker, not a residential one.

As you read on, you will find that I use many real estate and financing terms. If you are unfamiliar with their meaning, I have provided clear definitions for them in the "Glossary of Commercial Real Estate Terms" in the back of this book.

Finally, you should know that my more than thirty-five years of real estate experience is skewed toward the apartment side of real estate. I have financed and owned other property types over the years, but apartments are my first love. Some of the material here reflects my apartment background more so than other property types, but the principles I discuss translate to all real estate, not just to apartments. So regardless of your property loves or interests, you will find the help you need here.

Part 1

Buying Commercial
Real Estate

Why Invest in Commercial Real Estate?

The goal of retirement is to live off your assets, not on them.
–Frank Eberhart, author

Why should you invest in real estate, especially since there are many other types of assets to choose from? There is one overpowering reason to do so, but before I tell you what it is, I want to explain the benefits of owning commercial real estate.

FOUR WELL-KNOWN REASONS

When comparing commercial real estate to owning most other types of investments, there are four distinct advantages:

1. The positive cash flow from real estate is a major advantage over owning most other types of investment. Stocks and bonds can also provide positive cash flow from their dividends. Bonds much more so than stocks, as an average dividend yield on the New York Stock Exchange is about 2 percent. But well managed CRE should generate significantly better cash flow, conservatively 6 to 8 percent and higher is not uncommon.

2. 1031 exchanges on the sale of investment properties allow investors to defer capital gains taxes for decades. But if you sell another type of investment, you pay the capital gains that year.

3. Depreciation on real estate shelters income, reducing the investor's income tax burden. No such tax benefit exists for owning other asset classes.

4. Using debt to buy property substantially increases an investor's cash-on-cash return. How this happens will be explained in greater detail later in the book, but for now realize that modestly leveraging a property with debt can significantly improve its return on investment. This is a huge advantage of owning CRE over other types of investments.

These four reasons for owning real estate are commonly known benefits, but there are also three not so obvious reasons why investing in real estate is far superior to owning other types of investment assets. In my comments below, I will specifically focus on comparing real estate to owning stocks, because for many investors that is the logical alternative investment to owning real estate. But I believe this comparison is true of most other types of investments, not just owning equities.

THREE NOT SO OBVIOUS REASONS

The first less obvious reason to invest in real estate rather than owning stock has to do with the concept of efficient vs. inefficient markets. In an *efficient* market, everyone has the same financial information. And you buy at whatever the price is. The stock market is a good example of an efficient market. Investors know the value of each stock, and they have no legal way to buy a stock below the established market price.

The real estate market, on the other hand, is a perfect example of an *inefficient* market. The price of a piece of property is determined by what the seller and buyer agree upon. It has very little to do with the market at large. You make me an offer, and if I agree to it, we have a deal. It's as simple as that.

It is far more advantageous to invest in an inefficient market because you may have information that the seller doesn't, and this can make your investment worth much more than what the seller thinks it is worth. This happens all the time. The buyer sees a for-sale listing through a different set of eyes than the seller. He sees the property, not as it is, but for what it has the potential to become. Now the seller has decided it's time to sell, for whatever reason. He doesn't see the property's potential. Instead he sees the issues that plague his property. Who has the more accurate assessment of the property? No one knows with certainty, even when the sales price is agreed to between seller and buyer. But over time, the property's true potential will become readily apparent.

So the first not so obvious advantage of owning real estate over owning common stock is that it's possible to buy real estate at a bargain price. You can never buy stock at a bargain, only at what is considered the market price.

The second not so obvious reason to invest in real estate rather than owning other types of investments is that real estate owners have considerable influence on the outcome of their investments. They can:

1. make capital improvements to tired properties,
2. change management for those properties that are poorly managed, and
3. re-tenant properties with better quality and higher paying tenants.

As an owner of stock, you're a passive investor with no influence whatsoever on the value of your investment. You are truly a passive investor. You are at the whim of the emotions that control the stock market. Your particular stock might be doing well right now, but if the market takes a downward cycle, your stocks are going down in price with the rest of the market.

But the successful CRE investor is actively engaged with considerable influence on the value of his investment through a variety of ways. In commercial real estate, you actually have quite a bit of control over your investment and its potential for growth.

Finally, the third less obvious reason to invest in real estate versus stocks is no more need for retirement calculators. Yes, you heard me right, and here's why I say this. You've likely seen the television commercials where people are asked how much money they think they need to save over their lifetime in order to retire comfortably. Their response is typically a shrug of the shoulders, a bewildered look, a financial guess, a "beats me," or something equivalent. If your investments are in stocks, bonds, undeveloped land, precious metals, or other commodities, then a guess is about the best answer you can give. Who knows where these markets will be in ten years, twenty years, or thirty? It's anybody's guess, including the investment banking firm that produced the TV commercial.

But this is not so with commercial real estate. You can make a reasonable estimate as to how much you'll need to have accumulated in real estate in order to retire comfortably. All you need to know are the answers to these three basic questions:

1. How much annual income before taxes do you need to retire comfortably?
2. When you retire, how much are you expecting to receive annually from social security or other pensions you will receive?
3. What is the current cash-on-cash return you're receiving on your real estate investments?

For example, let's assume that you want $100,000 a year in income before taxes to live comfortably. As you get close to retirement age, the Social Security Administration sends you an annual letter stating what you will receive from them when you retire. Let's assume you and your spouse will receive a total of $40,000 annually from social security.

Now, to determine your current cash-on-cash return on your real estate investments, add up all owner disbursements you received last year on your rental properties and then divide by the total initial cash investment in all of your properties. Depending on how good an investor you are, that could be anything, but I believe a 6- to 8-percent cash-on-cash return is a conservative estimate on well managed properties. So for discussion purposes, let's assume your commercial real estate portfolio had a 6 percent cash-on-cash return last year. Now, let's do the math:

$100,000	Annual pretax income required
($40,000)	Less received from social security
$60,000	Net income needed from CRE investments
6.0%	Required return on your CRE investments
$1,000,000	Equity in CRE investments

Dividing $60,000 by 6 percent results in $1 million you will need to invest to make up the shortfall from your social security checks. In other words, over your lifetime, you will need to slowly grow your real estate investments until you have $1 million invested. If you are just starting out investing in real estate, this sounds like an enormous sum. But in reality, with prudent investing, this amount is attainable, in fact, quite likely to reach.

So, in this example, in order to live comfortably, you will need to have invested $1 million in real estate generating on average a 6 percent cash-on-cash return. If you do, you will never have to worry about running out of money as long as your properties are generating 6 percent annually.

What happens if high inflation hits? If your rents over time increase with the rate of inflation, you'll be fine. Living off the cash flow of your real estate portfolio means you never need to sell your properties to maintain your lifestyle. In fact, over time, your properties will continue to appreciate, increasing your equity even further in the years ahead.

THE BOTTOM-LINE

Real estate investing gives you an opportunity for financial freedom that owning stocks and other types of investment cannot. Those who invest in the stock market or other investment assets have a legitimate concern that they may outlive their money. Most other investment assets do not generate passive income, or if they do, they only yield a very modest return. In order to live off these other types of investment assets, retirees have to slowly sell them to maintain their lifestyle. Over time, their investment assets are sold. They live with a real fear that they may outlive their money. In contrast, once your real estate investments generate enough cash flow to maintain your lifestyle, you could live to be one hundred and twenty years old and still have no worries about running out of money. Congratulations, you have achieved financial freedom, something very few people will ever attain. Bottom-line, that's why investing in real estate is better than owning any other type of investment.

2

The Right Time to Invest

*I will tell you how to become wealthy. Be fearful when
others are greedy.
Be greedy when others are fearful.*
–Warren Buffett, billionaire investor

We would all be better investors, regardless of the type of investment we choose, if we understood two foundational truths about when is the optimal time to risk our hard earned money.

#1 - Sow seeds of success in the downtimes

A wise man once said, "The season of failure is the best time for sowing the seeds of success." I have found that when the real estate market is in a season of failure (recall the downturn that happened in 2008 and 2009), that is when you need to sow your seeds of success. Looking back, the Great Recession was a golden age for CRE investing.

In the summer of 2009, I was approached by a real estate investor about teaming up with him in purchasing a recently foreclosed apartment. Even during the recession, this property had remained fully occupied. The bank had an asking price of $39,000 per unit. Yes, the property needed modest amounts of renovations, but on paper it appeared to make a lot of sense. Like almost everyone else, though, my emotions were saying no. Fortunately, I didn't listen to my emotions. I, along with a group of other investors, purchased the property. Today it is conservatively worth $125,000 per unit. Over the years, my owner distributions have more than tripled my original investment in the property, and the property continues to cash flow beautifully.

Understand this important truth: Those who buy when everyone else is selling usually end up the big winners. This is true of all types of investing, but it's especially true with commercial real estate. Individuals who bought real estate at the bottom of the market cycle during the tough years made out like bandits. As the saying goes, "You make your money when you buy, not when you sell." In other words, to be a successful investor requires buying commercial real estate at the right price, and the best time to find bargain prices is at the bottom of the market when it's the scariest time to invest.

#2 - Avoid sowing seeds of failure in the good times

But the corollary of this truth is unfortunately also true. It's during prosperous times that many investors sow seeds of failure. They do this when they act as if the good times will last forever and then make foolish investment decisions. They forget the tough times and the hard lessons they should have learned. They say during the bleak times, "Never again will I ..." only to have selective amnesia when the market turns around. Always remember what you learn, especially the lessons learned the hard way. And then live and invest according to those lessons. This approach will grow success in life—personally and professionally.

WHAT IS THE REAL ESTATE MARKET CYCLE?

I often get asked, "Is this the right time to invest in real estate?" It's a legitimate question. As capitalization rates have steadily declined and property values have rapidly increased, this question becomes ever more important to answer. Other insightful questions asked are: "When will the real estate market turn?" and "Has the market peaked?" All good questions.

Before we can answer these, we need to determine where we are on the real estate market cycle. You may be aware that the real estate market cycle is cyclical with four distinct phases: Recovery, Expansion, Hyper-Supply, and

Recession. The chart below shows these four phases and how each one impacts new construction and vacancy rates.

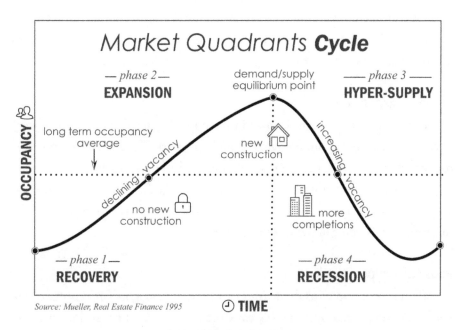

Cycle of Market Quadrants

Before I explain the four phases of the real estate market cycle, let's discuss the basics of the chart. The X axis (horizontal line at the bottom) represents Time and the Y axis (vertical line on the left) represents Occupancy. The horizontal dotted line in the middle represents the long-term average occupancy for the market. The vertical dotted line toward the middle represents when supply and demand are perfectly in balance. The black solid line that travels through all four quadrants represents the change in occupancy over time.

Now let's discuss the four quadrants.

Phase I - Recovery

The Recovery quadrant of the real estate market cycle (shown in the lower left-hand corner of the chart) is characterized by high vacancy and no new construction. Though it's not shown on this graph, generally rents are flat or declining during this phase. Owners offer rent concessions to avoid their property's occupancy rate from further declining.

The mood of investors in this quadrant begins with panic: *Oh, my, am I going to survive?* (recall market conditions in 2009). As the occupancy rate improves to the market's long-term average occupancy rate, investor attitude slowly turns to one of relief: *Whew, I made it through the worst of the market.*

Phase II – Expansion

The Expansion quadrant (shown in the upper left-hand corner of the chart) is characterized by declining vacancy and the start of new construction. As occupancy improves, concessions are eliminated and rent growth begins.

The mood of investors turns from relief—*I dodged a bullet*—to giddiness as vacancy rates decline and rents increase dramatically. Life is extremely good for investors at this point in the real estate cycle.

Phase III – Hyper-Supply

The Hyper-Supply quadrant (shown in the upper right-hand corner of the chart) is characterized by more new construction, and for the first time in a long time, vacancy rates begin to rise. Rent growth, though still positive, grows at a slower pace. And some neighborhoods start to experience rent concessions as new product that has recently come on line becomes increasingly more difficult to lease.

The investor mood turns from giddiness to one of caution and then denial that there is a problem brewing. The glass half full type of investors are still confident everything is going to work out just fine. They are thinking, *The slow rent up is only a bump in the road that will self-correct as long as I don't panic.*

Phase IV – Recession

The Recession quadrant (see the lower right-hand corner of the chart) is characterized by the completion of more and more product, which results in a substantial decline in occupancy rates. Newly completed product is sitting there unoccupied so developers begin running "blue light specials" to get them rented up. Concessions are abundant. Even investors with established properties are forced to offer concessions to avoid wholesale move outs.

In this phase, investor mood goes from denial to one of outright panic. Developers begin to wonder, *Am I going to make it?* The truth is, some will not. Also, some investors who recently bought properties at premium prices and then loaded them with lots of debt realize their mistake. Because they are leveraged to the hilt, a small drop in vacancy results in properties that no longer generate positive cash flow.

These are the four phases of the real estate market cycle. Understanding where the real estate market is on the cycle is critical to successful investing. Is the market climbing closer to a market peak or is it starting down the slippery slope to recession? How we answer this question may determine the difference between a successful investment or an albatross hanging around our necks.

So where are we today in the real estate market cycle? For the past several years (2013–2016), most real estate pundits have described the real estate market as being in Phase II, the Expansion Phase, which is characterized by high rent growth in a tight rental market. This time period can be best described by a quote from former Federal Reserve Chairman Alan Greenspan. He called it "irrational exuberance" when describing a euphoric stock market. I use a highly technical term to describe this part of the real estate cycle. I call it "The Silly-Stupid Phase."

WHAT IS THE CYCLE OF MARKET EMOTIONS?

Describing the real estate market as being in the Expansion Phase is kind of a Mr. Spock approach to evaluating market trends—all logic and no emotion. But emotions play a huge role in the real estate cycle. A useful tool called the Cycle of Market Emotions helps us understand how market phases are interconnected with prevailing moods, such as optimism, excitement, fear, panic, and hope. Imagine an emotional rollercoaster, and you'll get the idea.

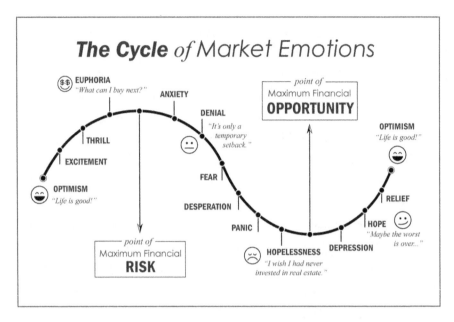

When the real estate market is at the very top of the incline, the predominant emotions are thrill and then euphoria. This happened in 2016. And when it does occur, you can almost hear a big brass band playing "Happy Days Are Here Again." During times such as these, investors in the real estate market usually have good justification for euphoria. Rents typically increase, sometimes dramatically, interest rates may hit new lows and remain there for some time, and developers may be slow to meet the demand. These conditions are great for investor return, both in appreciation of property values and increases of cash-on-cash returns. So why do I call this phase in the market the Silly-Stupid Phase?

Two Factors Fuel the Silly-Stupid Phase

The Silly-Stupid Phase is characterized by two factors. The first factor is cap rate compression. Cap rate compression happens when a real estate market gets stronger (i.e., investors are more confident) and the perceived risk of owning a rental property declines. Ken Griggs, president of the Real Estate Research Corporation, has talked about the precarious balance of value versus price in real estate. When assessing a most recent market condition, he said, "Our analysis showed upward pressure on pricing without a corresponding increase in value." That's a little scary. Now why does this happen? I believe buyers get caught up in the euphoria. They act as if this particular phase in the real estate cycle will continue forever. So they justify their price hikes, assuming rents will continue to rise and that their unrealistic pro forma projections will come to pass. But eventually, rents top out and vacancies start to rise.

The second factor associated with the Silly-Stupid Phase is lender aggressiveness. What I have observed and my lending peers confirm is that outlier lending institutions provide rates and terms that are significantly better than what is typically offered by most lenders. They aren't just competing for the business. In some instances, they outright buy it. And the larger financial institutions start offering rates and terms that are reminiscent of the years prior to the Great Recession—namely, interest-only loans, higher loan-to-value ratios, lower debt coverage ratios, and compressing of their spreads on interest rates. They hope that offering these "blue light specials" will help them hit their loan quotas. You may be thinking, *Why should I care if lenders are bending over backwards for my business? Let them. I don't have to accept what they are offering.* You're right. You don't. My advice is for you to take advantage of all these very favorable loan terms as long as you don't overleverage your properties. When the market turns— and it inevitably will—make sure that your rental property can support the mortgage payment when vacancy rates rise to levels associated with the bottom of the real estate cycle. This way you can protect yourself and your property investment.

Are We in the Hyper-Supply Phase of the Real Estate Market?

So where are we today in the real estate cycle? Since I'm most knowledgeable about commercial real estate in the Pacific Northwest, I'll speak to this question using the world I know best. As I have explained, the real estate cycle moves in definable phases, and while timing is a bit unpredictable, I believe the evidence suggests that in 2018 we are at the beginning of Phase III, the Hyper-Supply Phase. Here's why:

➢ After double-digit rent increases the past couple of years, rents are beginning to level off. They are still rising but much more modestly.

> ➤ As of this writing, construction is booming throughout the Pacific Northwest. Seattle and Portland are experiencing record amounts of construction. Seattle has more cranes dotting the skyline than any other city in the country. Portland has $2.5 billion worth of new development under construction. This was the single largest amount of construction in the Portland area ever, easily eclipsing the previous high of $1.9 billion set in 2016.

> ➤ For the first time in a long time, rent concessions are being offered on new product.

These three factors are all classic indicators that the market is in Phase III, the Hyper-Supply Phase.

So for the moment, let's assume that the real estate market is, in fact, in this quadrant of the real estate market cycle. Does this mean that investors should stop buying real estate right now? Heck no. If you know of future development that will have a positive influence on the property's neighborhood that the seller is not aware of, or you have a vision for how to turn a property from a loser to a winner, it makes little difference what phase of the market cycle we are currently in. You can still make a good investment. Even so, it's still important to understand that some phases of the real estate cycle are more difficult for profitable investing than others. If we truly are in the beginning of the downward real estate market cycle, then I advise that you proceed with caution. Don't be one of the Pollyanna investors who throws caution to the wind. Be prudent. Be alert for sudden changes in the market. If you do, you'll increase your chances for success.

THREE QUESTIONS BEFORE YOU DECIDE TO INVEST

So when is the right time to buy real estate? You need to start by asking yourself these questions:

1. *What is my time horizon? Do I have less than ten years before retirement?* If so, it may be best to invest in assets that are more liquid than commercial real estate and therefore easier to sell.

2. *What is my risk tolerance? Can I afford to lose money if the real estate market goes in the tank?* If not, it may be prudent to invest your money in lower-risk investments.

3. *Will I need the equity I accumulate in my real estate portfolio for other more important pursuits within the next few years? Or can I leave it alone and let it work for me?*

How you answer these questions will largely determine the correct course of action for you to follow.

Here are some reasons that may help you decide whether you should buy investment properties:

Good Reasons to Buy

➤ Ideally, the best time to buy is when it's a buyers market—that is, when the "herd" is selling.

➤ Buy when you've identified a replacement property for a potential 1031 exchange that has more upside than the property you currently own.

➤ Buy when you find a property with rents that are significantly below market value.

➤ Buy when you find a property that is being poorly managed resulting in a significantly higher vacancy rate than the overall market.

➤ Buy when you have a vision to improve a property that the current owner does not see.

➤ Buy when you see the property's neighborhood is in the path of growth.

Good Reasons Not to Buy

➤ Don't buy because everyone else is buying. Fight the urge to follow the herd. Don't be a lemming. Be patient. Those who buy when it's a sellers market are forced to pay top dollar for acquiring the property.

➤ Don't buy if your investment analysis shows the return on your equity is unacceptable. Don't assume that rising rents over time will bail out your poor return.

Even with all the cautions I've shared, finding good real estate deals is always possible. There will always be sellers who poorly manage their properties. There will always be sellers who don't know the real value of their properties. Often it just takes an investor who can bring the right vision and new management to the property to raise its value to the next level. And there isn't any good reason why that real estate investor with the right vision can't be *you*!

In the next chapter, I will share the real estate principles that will help you become a master of the art of commercial real estate investing.

3

Time-Proven Principles of Investing

Success leaves clues. People who succeed at the highest level are not lucky; they're doing something differently than everyone else does.

–Tony Robbins, author, life coach, inspirational speaker

James Montier, the author of the well-known book *The Little Book of Behavioral Investing*, wrote a white paper called "The Seven Immutable Laws of Investing." In his thesis, he identifies seven principles for sensible investing in the stock or bond markets. I was intrigued by the title, so I read the article and somewhere along the way realized that six of these seven "immutable laws of investing" also apply to investing in commercial real estate.

THE SIX IMMUTABLE LAWS OF CRE INVESTING

1. Always insist on a margin of safety

In other words, the goal is not to buy at fair market value but to purchase with a margin of safety because property performance, market conditions, and the like may not live up to expectations. This means finding a property that is underperforming in the market, but, with a change in ownership, the property's performance will turn around.

17

2. This time is never different

The four most dangerous words in investing are "This time is different." The dot.com bubble that occurred from 1999 to 2001 is a perfect example. Investors were buying stock in companies that hadn't turned a profit because they expected these companies would become the next Google or Amazon.com. Stock prices soared, and even though it made no logical sense, the contention that was bandied about was "this time is different." The same was true of real estate prior to the Great Recession. Many people believed that house prices could never go down, that we had hit a new permanent high. In both examples, however, a speculative fever resulted in a bubble that caused stocks and house prices to plummet in value.

Whenever someone starts saying, "This time it's different," get out of that investment as quickly as you can.

3. Be patient and wait for the fat pitch

Mr. Montier states in his white paper: "Patience is integral to any value-based approach on many levels. … However patience is in rare supply." In commercial real estate, there is a time to wait and a time to act. When things go bad, like what occurred after the Great Recession, the tendency is to dump our rental properties as quickly as we can. But the prudent thing to do is wait.

Most investors suffer from an "action bias"—a desire to do something. But often the best thing to do is to stand at the plate and wait for the "fat pitch." A "fat pitch" is a baseball analogy where the pitcher is behind in the count and his next pitch needs to be a strike or he's walking the batter. He knows that, and more importantly the batter knows that. So the batter just patiently waits for that fat pitch that he can hit for extra bases. Likewise, real estate investors need to be patient as they look for those buying opportunities that will be home runs for them.

4. Be contrarian

Humans are prone to the herd instinct. Investors are often no exception. When everyone is buying, investors typically buy; when everyone is selling, they sell.

In 2009, during the worst of the recession, a group of us put under contract an apartment that had been foreclosed on by the lender. It took me six months to find a lender who would finance this property. Today, the property is by far my best investment. The value has shot up dramatically, and the property is truly a cash cow.

Are all the bargains gone in a high-priced market? I don't believe so, but finding them is certainly more challenging. Anytime can be a good time to buy. But if you go along with the herd and sit on the sidelines with them, you may miss out on some of the best deals to be had.

5. Be leery of leverage

As an investor, I'm always trying to improve my property's cash-on-cash return. Adding modest amounts of debt to be paid from the property's cash flow is the easiest way to substantially improve its cash-on-cash return. Why? As you add debt, you reduce the equity invested in the property. Counter balancing reduced equity is an incremental reduction in the property's cashflow after debt service resulting from the monthly mortgage payment modestly increasing. So leverage can positively influence the property's cash-on-cash return. But there is a limit, and we investor's need to be very leery of leveraging our properties too much. In many instances, those owners with properties that were over-leveraged in 2008 paid the ultimate price—the loss of their properties. Those homeowners prior to the Great Recession who used their homes as ATM machines learned the hard way too. Seven million homeowners lost their homes to foreclosure during the last recession.

6. Never invest in something you don't understand

This is just plain old common sense. All too often, I have found myself talking with commercial real estate investors who are clueless about their property holdings. This puts them at the mercy of their real estate advisors. Many times these advisors have a different agenda than the owner, but the owner, not knowing the fundamentals of CRE, is unaware of the conflict of interest. It's a simple truth: If you don't understand the investment concept, then you shouldn't be investing in it.

As long as you follow these six fundamental principles of CRE investing, you can be confident you're investing wisely. Otherwise, you can go through life being part of the herd, following the latest trend only to be sadly mistaken when the real estate market turns.

FIVE HABITS OF HIGHLY SUCCESSFUL CRE INVESTORS

Over the past thirty years, I have had the opportunity to work with many commercial real estate investors. What I've noticed is that highly successful CRE investors have several habits in common.

1. A Simple Approach to Analyzing Opportunities

Each investor has his own methods of analyzing a deal, but surprisingly most have a relatively simple set of parameters they use as guidelines for making their go/no-go decisions for purchasing commercial real estate. Rarely do they employ the more sophisticated methods of evaluation, such as Net Present Value (NPV) or Internal Rate of Return (IRR).

2. A Big Picture Approach to Investing

Successful CRE investors don't get caught up in the minutia of the deal. Rather, they step back and look at the big picture. Put another way, they get off the ground and fly thirty thousand feet above in order to effectively make the right decision. In many ways, their decision making is more of an art than a science. Because of it, they're able to pull the trigger much faster than those who over analyze their opportunities.

3. Listen to a Core Group of Advisors

Some successful CRE investors go it alone, relying solely on their own expertise. But most have a team of advisors. These investors realize that their area of expertise, though valuable, is limited, which requires that they rely on the proven counsel of others in order to reduce the risk of making a poor investment decision.

They usually have no more than two to four advisors making up their group. These advisors are considered an invaluable part of the investor's team, and many times these advisors become minority owners in the transaction. The successful investor has learned over the years to trust his team's wise counsel in their specific area of expertise.

4. Regularly Monitor Investments

Successful investors vary greatly on how involved they are in the day-to-day affairs of their properties. Some are totally hands-on. They enjoy the property management side of the business. Most delegate the daily decisions to a property management company. But all highly successful real estate investors closely monitor their properties' monthly operating statements. They believe in the saying, "You get what you inspect, not what you expect." They usually focus on two or three metrics, such as the vacancy rate, capital repairs, and the last time rents were raised.

5. Always Seek New Opportunities

A common theme among successful real estate investors is that they are *always* in the market for new opportunities. They continually keep their eyes and ears open for another good investment. The point of this habit is that, whether they are in the market to buy more properties or not, they want others to consider them a serious player, so when the right property comes along, they will be notified of the opportunity.

Bottom-line: Highly successful CRE investors don't just invest in real estate; they *live* real estate. *It's their passion.* They can't think of anything they would rather do than to hunt for the next deal.

PRACTICES TO REDUCE THE RISK OF CRE INVESTING

Investing in commercial real estate is without a doubt a high risk and high reward venture. Lots of money can be made in real estate. Just talk to those who had the courage and foresight to acquire income-producing properties just after the Great Recession. Those properties that were bought at bargain-basement prices more than doubled in value within five or so years.

In contrast, talk to those investors who owned overpriced and over-leveraged properties prior to the Great Recession. How many of these properties ended up going back to the lender? How many investors filed for bankruptcy when their properties, with vacancies rising, no longer cash flowed? So it goes both ways: high risk, high reward, *and* unfortunately, sometimes you can lose everything.

But there are things that you, the investor, can do to significantly reduce the risk of CRE investing. You will never be able to eliminate the risk, but I believe you can reduce it to a manageable level. Here's how.

➢ **Become an expert in one particular property type.** Each type of property has its own unique idiosyncrasies. Learning the nuances of a specific property type increases your chances of being a successful CRE investor.

➢ **Don't be afraid to deviate from the crowd.** The herd mentality usually results in poor long-term investment results. If you have well thought-out investment criteria that run counter to the prevailing view, don't be afraid to chart a different course than the rest of the pack.

➢ **Know intimately your geographic market.** Know the macroeconomics of the metropolitan area you're investing in. More importantly, know which neighborhoods are better than others. Understand the long-term growth patterns. Learn which neighborhoods are going to be the up-and-coming areas of the city over the next ten years.

➢ **Use objective measurements to determine the worthiness of buying a property**. Whether you use a Cash-on Cash analysis, Internal Rate of Return, Net Present Value, or some other criteria, live and die by it. Don't get sucked into someone else's method of determining the value of an investment. And don't use subjective criteria that have no rational basis to them—for example, buying a "trophy type" property that looks great but is so overpriced it would be better if you invested your money in bonds with a yield of 2 percent. Use whatever objective criteria makes sense to you and then stick to them.

➢ **Never ever use the seller's pro forma for evaluating an investment**. Assume that all sellers and listing brokers are going to inaccurately skew the projected income and expenses in their favor so as to maximize the property's value. There is a good reason why at the bottom of the listing broker's marketing flyers the following statement (or something similar) is provided: *This information supplied herein is from sources we deem reliable. It is provided without any representations, warranty or guarantee, expressed or implied as to its accuracy. Prospective Buyer should conduct an independent investigation and verification of all matters deemed to be material, including, but not limited to, statements of income and expenses. CONSULT YOUR ATTORNEY, ACCOUNTANT, OR OTHER PROFESSIONAL ADVISOR.* These capitalized letters are theirs, not mine. I rarely receive the listing broker's marketing package where the rents weren't overstated or the operating expenses weren't understated—or both. Always ask for the actual operating statements for the past three years and a current rent roll. Base your numbers on the historical operating statements, not on the marketing package.

➤ **Buy properties with a potential to add value.** Let's face it. At the time I am writing this book, we are in the real estate cycle quadrant where properties for sale are overvalued. So if you are buying a property in such a market, you are buying a property close to the top of the market. There are only two ways to make money on real estate at such inflated prices: either (1) have a long-term hold strategy (ten years or longer), or (2) find properties that have the potential to add value. Generally, "value-add" properties have some type of "hair" on them. Solve the issue, and you'll be rewarded with a substantial increase in the property's value.

➤ **Choose a property management company that specializes in your property type, your property's size, and its geographic location.** For example, let's say you buy an eighty-unit apartment complex. Find a property management company that specializes in apartments, has several apartments under management in that size range, and manages properties within close proximity to your property. Doing so increases your chances that the property management company selected has the appropriate management experience and is knowledgeable about the property's neighborhood.

➤ **Remember, you get what you inspect, not what you expect.** Some will tell you that owning real estate is a passive investment. For most property types, that's a myth. If you want to maximize your chances of getting a good return on your commercial real estate, you must be proactive in overseeing your properties. Even if you hire a quality property management company, they are too busy with the day-to-day operations of the property to do much more than "put out fires." Quite frankly, they don't get paid enough to do more than that. So it is imperative that you regularly inspect your property to make sure something is not being overlooked. And you need to regularly review the property's operating statements and ask questions when something doesn't make sense to you.

> **Don't over-leverage your properties.** Take advantage of all the "blue light specials" that lenders offer—except for one: don't over-leverage your properties. Those investors with over-leveraged properties at the beginning of the Great Recession can tell you that if they had it to do over again, they would have been far more conservative with their use of debt.

FIVE MISTAKES TO AVOID WHEN BUYING RENTAL PROPERTIES

Shown below are five real estate investing mistakes I've seen committed repeatedly over the years. Avoid these blunders at all costs.

Mistake 1 – Analysis by Paralysis: Getting Bogged Down in the Minutia

This type of investor believes that the more information he gets on the property, the better will be his purchasing decision. Unfortunately, in most instances, that's not the case. As the saying goes, these investors "Can't see the forest for the trees." They are so involved in the details of the purchase that they forget the big picture. Savvy real estate investors don't get caught up in the minutia. They generally focus on a small subset of issues to get comfortable with determining whether or not they'll make an offer on a property.

Not only does analysis by paralysis complicate the buying decision, it also lengthens the time necessary to come to a decision. Many times another buyer comes along, while Mr. Analysis-by-Paralysis continues slogging through his analysis, and steals the property away from him. In reality, the seller is tired of all the nitpicky questions the original buyer has bombarded her with. She is relieved someone else is swooping in to save her from the buyer who can't get too much information on the property.

Mistake 2 – Doing Only a Cursory Due Diligence on the Property

Opposite of Mr. Analysis-by-Paralysis is the investor who does only a cursory due diligence on the property. This usually takes two forms. The first mistake is not reviewing the historical operating statements and current rent roll carefully. It's not uncommon for a property's profit and loss statement to be difficult to fully grasp for the average reader. Lots of important information can be hidden in the property's operating statements. They need to be teased out by asking the seller good, penetrating questions. For example:

➢ If it's not obvious, ask the seller what the vacancy rate has been over the last three years.

➢ Why did a particular operating expense increase or decrease dramatically last year compared to previous years?

➢ Are there one-time expenses in the operating expenses that should be removed from the projected operating budget?

➢ Why haven't the rents increased to market for all the tenants shown on the rent roll?

Those are a few questions that may be appropriate to ask.

The second mistake is only doing a cursory physical inspection of the property. If you're buying apartments, you need to have your building inspector check every unit, the roofs, the laundry areas, the attics, the crawlspaces, and so on. Don't cut corners when it comes to the physical inspection of the property. Find a well-qualified inspector to represent you who will provide a detailed report of the property's physical condition.

Mistake 3 – Lacking a Consensus among the Investors about Their Investing Strategy for the Property

If you are buying a property with a group of investors, make sure those who are in the investor group have the same goals and exit strategy as you do. It's not uncommon to find out, after it's too late, that individuals in the investor group have motivations for owning the property that differ from yours.

> ➢ Some may want to fix it and flip it. Others may want to hold the property long term.
> ➢ Some may want to have maximum leverage. Others may want to have modest leverage in order to maximize cash flow.
> ➢ Some may want to refinance at the earliest possible opportunity to take cash out. Others may want to pay down the loan over time.
> ➢ Some may want to invest more dollars in maintaining or upgrading the property. Others may prefer to do less capital repairs and take more cash out of the property.

Before you decide to be in an investor group that is purchasing a property, have a meeting with the potential investors. Ask the managing member of the LLC to outline his goals and exit strategy for the property. Also get a feel for whether you would want to be stuck with these investors over the investment life of the property. If you don't like what you hear from the managing member of the LLC or your gut tells you not to invest with one of the investors in the group, pass on the opportunity. It's better that you walk away from the opportunity than later regret accepting it.

Mistake 4 – Lack of Cash Reserves for Unexpected Expenses

One of the biggest mistakes investors make is not having sufficient cash reserves available for unexpected expenses. This is especially true for multi-tenanted office and retail properties. For example, a short-sighted investor owns a multi-tenanted office building. He has owned the building for years, and it has cash flowed beautifully. But instead of putting some of the positive cash flow into a reserve account for future needs, he puts it all into his back pocket. Then one day one of his larger tenants moves out and the property no longer cash flows like it once did. Now the owner has to contribute his own cash to keep the mortgage current. He would like to get the vacant space market ready, but to do the generic tenant improvements and pay a leasing commission will cost him more money than he has in his savings. So the space remains vacant because he tries to do the leasing himself to avoid paying a leasing commission. Over time the property deteriorates because he can't afford to maintain it. Years go by and the loan comes due. Because the property no longer cash flows, the owner has three choices, none of which he wants to do: (1) he can pay down the loan so the property can achieve the lender's minimum debt coverage requirement; (2) he can sell the property at a discount because no one will buy a nonperforming property at a reasonable price; or (3) he can give the property back to the lender.

This scenario happened repeatedly during the Great Recession. And the sad thing is, it didn't need to. If owners had established a reserve account for the eventual cost of tenant improvements and leasing commissions, they would have had the funds to get their properties re-tenanted.

Mistake 5 – Paying More Than the Property Is Worth to Avoid Capital Gains Taxes

A 1031 exchange allows investors to defer their capital gains tax when they reinvest their equity into a like kind-exchange. Deferring the payment of your capital gains taxes to a later date is a *huge* advantage to real estate investors. But sometimes investors are so eager not to pay their capital gains taxes that they pay way too much for their exchange property.

If you can find an exchange property at a market price, then do a 1031 exchange. But first find out what the capital gains taxes would be if you didn't do a 1031 exchange. No one likes to pay the IRS if they don't have to. I get that. But don't get silly-stupid about the price of the exchange property. Sometimes it is better to pay your capital gains tax than to get stuck with a property that will never be a good investment because you paid too much for it.

INVESTOR MUTINY IGNORES FIVE TRUTHS ABOUT REINVESTING

Have you ever been caught between two highly contentious factions with your personal vote determining who wins and who loses? To make matters worse, whichever side doesn't get your vote considers you their enemy. That unfortunately happened to me once. It's no fun being caught in the middle. But I apologize, since I'm starting in the middle of this true story. Let me start this time from the beginning.

I was one of seven CRE investors who formed an LLC to purchase a run-down apartment. The previous owner had died, and the heirs to his estate had no interest in the property so it slowly deteriorated. Eventually they decided to sell. By the time my investor group acquired the property, it was sorry looking.

During our first year of ownership, the renovation of the property proceeded at a slower pace and at a higher cost than we had originally anticipated. Some investors were disappointed in the progress and had no qualms making their opinions known.

Well into the second year, the property had not yet provided any ownership distributions, causing growing dissension among the investors. (Ownership distributions are the excess cash flows generated from the operations of the rental property that can be safely distributed back to the owners based on their percentage of ownership in the property.) An owners' meeting was called by those who wanted to oust the managing member of the LLC as well as the property management company. All the owners were present as well as a representative of the property management company. Civility soon gave way to finger-pointing and name-calling. The management company representative finally walked out after a heated exchange. I've never before been in a meeting this contentious.

A vote was called, and eventually everyone realized I had the deciding vote.

All eyes were on me.

How would I vote?

Actually, my decision regarding which side to support was an easy one. There were five reasons I voted in favor of retaining both the managing member of the LLC and the property management company. In my view, these five reasons are timeless commercial real estate investing principles that all of us who in invest in CRE should follow.

Principle 1 – Have realistic expectations

Investing in commercial real estate requires patience. Nothing happens quickly. In a value-added acquisition, especially one that was in as poor condition as this property was, it was not reasonable to expect owner distributions of any amount in the first couple of years.

Principle 2 – Focus on long-term benefits, not short-term gains

The real priority was not near-term cash flow, but how well was the property going to operate after the renovation? Specifically:

➢ How much cash flow would be generated in three to five years?
➢ How much would the property appreciate after improving the tenant profile?

This is where the focus should have been.

Principle 3 – Focus on growing income, not cutting costs

The cost of gopher extermination was one of the reasons the investors wanted to oust the property management company at the owners' meeting. I was thinking to myself, *You've got to be kidding me! Why get all hot and bothered by such a minor issue?* But they did. Those who focused on cutting costs didn't understand that turning a property around is all about growing the property's income, and that requires spending money, not cutting costs.

Principle 4 – Listen to the counsel of those who have commercial real estate investing experience

The managing member of the LLC had forty years of experience in real estate. He was not some newbie to real estate, and he had a distinguished track record. The LLC members wouldn't have even had the opportunity to invest in the property if he had not identified the property's potential investment opportunity. There is a time to challenge leadership, but eighteen months into a project is way too early to jump ship.

Principle 5 – Don't micromanage those who have decision-making authority

I applaud members of an LLC who ask probing questions to those who have the day-to-day responsibilities managing a property. But they need to allow those who have operational responsibility to do their job without the Monday-morning quarterbacking. Their philosophy should be to give those in charge of the daily affairs of the property enough rope to hang themselves. If sufficient time has elapsed and they're not performing up to your expectations, then and only then do you think about replacing those in charge.

After the vote, I received the heartfelt gratitude from those I sided with and the animosity of those I voted against. There was no way to reconcile differences, so as the weeks passed, I asked if I could buy out the two partners who had instigated the uprising. Both were eager to get out of the LLC, and we came to a mutually agreed-upon price for their interests in the property.

From the vantage point of time, I have no doubt that I made the right decision. We later refinanced the property, resulting in cash back to the owners that was slightly less than our original investment in the property. The appraised value of the property after the renovation nearly doubled from what we paid for it three years before, and the property is now yielding healthy monthly owner distributions.

The lesson I learned from this difficult experience was to trust these five time-proven principles of real estate investing.

FOUR LESSONS LEARNED FROM INVESTING IN MY LOSER PROPERTY

Not every commercial real estate property turns out to be a home run. My investments are no exception. Occasionally I strike out. But even then, there are lessons I have learned.

In the summer of 2007, which turned out to be the absolute peak of the last real estate cycle, I, along with a like-minded group of investors, purchased a thirty-two-unit apartment located in a small town. At the time, it seemed to be a good investment:

1. large-unit sizes;

2.   one-story buildings;

3.   situated in a nice, quiet, little town;

4.   with the potential down the road to convert to condominiums.

Hey, what could go wrong? I asked myself.

Well, it turns out that plenty could go wrong. And some of it could not have been predicted by even the most savvy of CRE investors. Because of that, I needed to extend mercy to myself instead of beating up myself over investing in this property.

In 2015, with a sigh of relief, we sold this apartment complex. For several weeks after, you could see me doing back flips as I celebrated the sale of this loser property.

Years have passed since. From the vantage point of time, I now realize I learned some invaluable lessons from that experience.

1.   **Market timing is everything.** The old adage, "You make your money on an investment when you purchase it, not when you sell it," is very true. This investment had very little chance to perform well because we simply paid too much for it. We bought this property at the peak of the real estate cycle. If we had purchased it a year or two earlier at a much less inflated price, this property would have likely performed admirably.

2.   **There's a reason why properties in small markets have higher cap rates.** When the economy went bust in 2008, unemployment soared, vacancy rates rose, and rents flattened or declined because of concessions. As bad as this was in the large metropolitan areas (think Portland, Seattle, or San Francisco), it was far worse in the small towns that had higher vacancy rates and struggled with more significant rent concessions. When the real estate market finally turned in the large cities, it was still another year or two before the small town our property was located in began to see occupancy rates rise and modest rent growth. This is what I learned: Buying properties in small markets at higher cap rates is not a bargain. There is more risk associated with rental properties in small towns, and they deserve a higher cap rate.

3. **Never underestimate the cost of deferred maintenance.** This property was purchased as a value-added play. We realized at the time we bought it that there was a lot of deferred maintenance that needed to be corrected. So when we purchased the property, we had what we thought was a sizeable war chest set aside for capital improvements. In reality, we weren't even close. Even though we sunk a lot of money in capital repairs into the property, I'm sure the buyer was thinking that all he had to do to make this property perform well was to tackle all of the deferred maintenance. What he didn't realize is that we had already invested a lot of money in the property. We finally decided that it was in our best interests to sell this property rather than continue pouring more money into capital improvements that may or may not positively grow rents.

4. **Pay close attention to your on-site manager.** During the eight years we owned the apartment, we had three different on-site managers (we had to fire the first two). Each started out well managing the property, but over time their performance was highly correlated to how well we monitored them. Once we began to trust how well they were managing the property, the property's performance began to slowly go downhill: vacancy rates rose, the grounds didn't look crisp and clean, and tenant evictions for nonpayment of rent lingered longer than they should have. But as soon as we started asking the on-site manager insightful questions about the property's performance and occasionally visited the property, things began to improve. Remember, you get what you inspect, not what you expect.

Take Heed, These Issues Could Happen to You

Why should you care that I learned these four lessons the hard way about investing in my loser property? Simply put, because the same types of issues could happen to you, especially when the commercial real estate market peaks. Some investors sense when this is occurring, while others ignore the signs. This second group of investors tend to do the following:

> ➤ Pay too much for properties, assuming that rents will continue to rise (a.k.a. lesson 1 above).
>
> ➤ Seek out more reasonably priced investments in tertiary markets, forgetting that there is a reason why cap rates are higher for these properties (a.k.a. lesson 2 above).
>
> ➤ Buying more value-added properties may or may not be a good investment decision. If you've never purchased a property with a lot of deferred maintenance, be very careful (a.k.a. lesson 3 above).

Sometimes the best CRE investment decision you can make is deciding not to buy. After doing a careful analysis of the property, sometimes the risks outweigh the benefits. It's far better to walk away than to invest in a property that is doomed from the outset. Heed my counsel. You'll be better off for it.

WARREN BUFFETT'S SURPRISING APPROACH TO REAL ESTATE INVESTING

Warren Buffett, the CEO of Berkshire Hathaway, has made his considerable fortune investing in the stock market. In 2016, *Fortune* magazine ranked him as the third wealthiest person on the planet, with a net worth approaching $80 billion. Not too shabby!

Unknown to most people are Mr. Buffett's two small real estate investments that he made long ago. Both have amply rewarded him for his willingness to invest outside his area of expertise. And far more important than their profitability were the five common sense principles he learned from his real estate investments.

In 1986, he purchased a four-hundred-acre farm located outside of Omaha, Nebraska. He purchased the farm from the Federal Deposit Insurance Corporation (FDIC) which had inherited it from a bank that failed. Mr. Buffett admits that he knows nothing about farming, but he has a son who loves to farm so he turned the day-to-day operations over to him. Mr. Buffett recognized that purchasing the farm was a good investment decision. As he said, "I needed no unusual knowledge or intelligence to conclude that the investment had no downside and potentially had substantial upside."

Three decades later, the farm tripled its earnings. As of this writing, the property is worth five times what he paid for it. Certainly, an excellent investment.

In 1993, Mr. Buffett purchased a retail property located adjacent to New York University that the Resolution Trust Corporation (RTC) was selling. A real estate bubble had popped, and the RTC had been created to dispose of assets of failed savings institutions. His investment analysis was very rudimentary. The property had been poorly managed by the previous owner and then by the RTC. The vacancy at the property was well above the market's vacancy rate for no apparent reason. The largest tenant's rent was five dollars per square foot compared to all the other tenants' rent averaging seventy dollars per square foot. Mr. Buffett realized that when the current lease term expired for this tenant, the new rent on this space would dramatically improve the property's cash flow. And like the time he purchased the farm, he realized that he needed to turn the management of the property over to an experienced property manager, which he did.

Over a relatively short period of time, the new property manager was able to lease the vacant space and raise to market level the rent on the building's largest tenant. As a result, the property's net cash flow tripled, and annual distributions as of 2017 exceeded 35 percent of Mr. Buffett's original investment.

So what has Mr. Buffett learned from his two real estate investments?

➢ Notice that he bought both properties out of foreclosure when the real estate market was at the bottom of the cycle. "I will tell you how to become wealthy," Mr. Buffett once said. "Be fearful when others are greedy. Be greedy when others are fearful." When he bought these two properties, most investors were out of the market, fearful that real estate wasn't ever going to turn around. Mr. Buffett knew differently and acted on it.

➢ You don't have to be a real estate expert to achieve satisfactory investment returns. But you do need to turn over management of the property to someone who is well qualified to manage the property for you.

➢ You don't need to do a sophisticated investment analysis to determine whether to purchase a property. Many times a common sense look at the property will do. Ask yourself, *What is holding this property back from operating well?* If you can answer this question and you're confident that you can correct the problem, then buy the property.

➢ Investing over the long term will eventually solve most problems. Notice, Mr. Buffett still owns these two properties. One he bought in 1986, and the other he bought in 1993. As he likes to say, "Our favorite holding period is forever."

➢ He didn't concern himself about either property's daily valuations. He understood that he bought the properties at bargain prices and that overtime they would make good investments. "Games are won by players who focus on the playing field," he quipped, "not by those whose eyes are glued to the scoreboard."

Now that you have an introductory understanding of what successful CRE investing principles look like, the next step is to develop your own CRE investing strategy that works best for you.

4

Do You Want to Be an Active or Passive Investor?

Now, one thing I tell everyone is learn about real estate.
Repeat after me: real estate provides the highest returns,
the greatest values and the least risk.
–Armstrong Williams, entrepreneur, political commentator

In the three previous chapters you've learned:

➤ That owning commercial real estate is a better investment than any other investment asset because it generates cash flow that has the potential to supplement your retirement income without eating into your real estate equity. Once your rental properties begin to generate the cash flow you need to maintain your lifestyle, you'll never have to worry about funding your retirement years! You can't say that about other types of investments.

➤ The importance of the Real Estate Cycle and the Cycle of Market Emotions on *when* to invest in commercial real estate.

➤ Several time-proven principles of how to invest in commercial real estate.

Consider these first three chapters as the foundation upon which to build your commercial real estate investment strategy.

DECIDING YOUR COMMERCIAL REAL ESTATE INVESTMENT STRATEGY

The next building block is actually deciding how actively involved you want to be in acquiring, financing, managing, and eventually selling your real estate. What you decide about your participation in the process runs the gamut from being actively involved in every important decision to being completely passive, making no day-to-day decisions about your property.

To help you choose the option that best fits you, here are some questions to answer.

Do you want to be an active or passive investor? Another way of looking at it is, do you want to make all of the decisions about the property, or do you want to defer the decision making to someone else?

Under both scenarios – active and passive, you have two choices to make. If you choose to be an *active* investor:

1. Do you want to be a solo investor working by yourself? Or
2. Do you want to be the decision maker—that is, the managing member for a group of passive investors who want to form a limited liability company for the purpose of investing in rental properties?

And if you decide you want to be a *passive* investor, where someone else makes the decisions:

1. Do you want to seek out a traditional real estate sponsor, someone who is well known in your community for his or her real estate acumen? Or
2. Do you want to use the services of an online crowdfunding platform to invest your money with?

There is no right or wrong choice. Either active or passive investing will get you where you want to go. Your choice depends on how involved you want to be in the process, how much risk you want to take on, and how much money you want to invest. Let's look at each of the alternatives.

Alternative 1 – Active Investor: Make the Decisions for You or the LLC

As an active investor, you will be making all the important decisions: what to buy, how much to offer, finding the lender, managing the property, to name just a few. Most investors who make this choice start by investing in duplexes or triplexes. As they gain confidence in their real estate acumen and additional equity in their real estate, they slowly increase the size of their real estate acquisitions.

The advantage of this approach is investors learn as they go. And when they make mistakes, they are relatively small and, in most instances, correctable. The disadvantage of this approach is that it requires a lot of time and effort on the investor's part.

Over the years, I've come to know many investors who have taken this approach to investing. Most of them gradually build wealth over time and are highly successful. But burnout is a real threat to this investing approach.

Alternative 2 – Passive Investor: Defer the Decisions to Someone Else

For most investors who have money to invest but realize they don't have the expertise or the interest or time to acquire and manage an income-producing property, they seek out an experienced real estate sage (sponsor) to latch onto. There is wisdom letting someone else do the heavy lifting of investing if that's not your strength. Whether you seek out a traditional real estate sponsor or decide to invest in a crowdfunding platform, you need to vet the sponsor you're placing your trust and your money in. Are they known for their integrity? Or are they like snake oil salesmen, to be avoided like the plague? Here are some things to consider when vetting your real estate investment expert.

Assess the sponsor's real estate experience

More experienced sponsors have a higher probability of success than beginners. So how many years of experience does your sponsor have investing in commercial real estate? What is his track record? Has he ever lost money in investing in real estate? How did he weather the Great Recession? Ask pointed, revealing questions.

Assess the sponsor's experience with the location

The sponsor may have an excellent real estate investment track record, but all of his experience may be located in one geographic region. Does he have any experience in the city where the investment is located in? Does he know this particular market?

Determine how much money your sponsor is investing in the property

A while back, I was asked to find financing for a property that had a nationally recognized property investment syndication firm as the managing member of the LLC. In the investment memorandum, they were providing a decent preferred return for their investors, but I was unable to determine how much money the syndicator was investing in the acquisition of the property. It was purposely vague. So I asked. The answer was *nothing*! They were receiving a very healthy fee from their investors for putting the deal together, and they were receiving excellent profits after the preferred return for the investor was achieved. But they were taking no risk whatsoever. If the property tanked, they would not lose a single dime. All the risk was shared between their investors and the lender who had the most to lose.

A sponsor with no "skin in the game" should not be considered a legitimate sponsor for investing your hard earned money. Drop them like a hot potato and find a sponsor who will risk his capital with you.

Carefully review the pro forma for conservative or aggressive assumptions

Your goal should be to understand whether you're dealing with conservative or aggressive assumptions. How do proposed rents compare to current market rents? Is the pro forma vacancy reasonable when compared to similar properties in the market area? Are proposed operating expenses in line with the historical operating expenses? If you're not able to answer these questions, find a third party that can, and pay them for their time and effort.

Review the profit splits

How are the monthly cash flows split between the investors and the sponsor? When the property is sold, how are the gains split? Some sponsors will offer the investor a preferred return. I'm not a fan of preferred returns, and here's why. An investor gives up something for receiving a preferred return: he limits his owner distributions from cash flow and the upside potential gain when the property is sold. I would rather not have a preferred return so that I receive at the time of sale my pro rata share of the cash flow and the pro rata share of the gain.

Review all legal documents

Have a competent real estate attorney review the Operating Agreement of the LLC or the Private Placement Memorandum. Can you understand the legalese? If not, ask questions until you do. Does this legal document divide up risk and reward appropriately, or does it inordinately favor the sponsor?

If you haven't already seen this, in time you will discover that some investors have invested with sponsors who have the morals of snake oil salesmen. Don't be a lemming running with the herd headlong into the ocean. Vet your sponsors to avoid this from happening to you.

INVESTING ONLINE THROUGH A CROWDFUNDING PORTAL

If you decide to invest online through a crowdfunding source, the vetting process goes beyond investigating the sponsor. You must also fully understand the crowdfunding process. Make no mistake, crowdfunding is here to stay, and it could have enormous influence on how commercial real estate is funded in the future. Some pundits are even predicting that crowdfunding has the potential to be a disruptive technology—a technology that helps create a new market that eventually disrupts the traditional way of doing business. But before I go further, let's start with the basics.[3]

What is crowdfunding?

Crowdfunding, as defined by the Massolution 2015CR-RE Crowdfunding for Real Estate Report, is "an Internet-facilitated means for sponsors, businesses, or other entities to raise funds from a multitude of individual investors or patrons, even institutions, for a particular project or initiative. For securities based transactions the outreach, or open call, is typically limited to accredited investors."

The crowdfunding concept of raising funds from a multitude of individual investors or patrons for a particular project has been around for a long time. For example, more than a hundred years ago, the base for the Statue of Liberty was financed by Americans donating small sums of money to the cause.

What makes crowdfunding unique?

What makes real estate crowdfunding unique from other forms of real estate investments is its use of the Internet and other technology to raise the needed funds.

Who is allowed to invest?

In the United States, only accredited investors are allowed to invest in crowdfunding. An accredited investor is someone who has a net worth of at least $1 million, not including the value of her primary residence, or has income of at least $200,000 annually for the last two years (or if married, $300,000 together with her spouse).

How many crowdfunding models are there?

There are four financial crowdfunding models:

1. **Lending** – Crowdfunders lend money to a sponsor, typically secured by real estate. In exchange they receive interest payments and a return of their original capital.
3. **Equity** – Crowdfunders invest their funds in a sponsor's property, and in return they receive ongoing cash flow and capital appreciation when the property is sold.
4. **Royalty** – Crowdfunders invest their funds and receive a usage-based payment from another party for that party's right to ongoing use of an asset, such as a percentage of rent from a lease.
5. **Hybrid** – This is a combination of two of the other three models.

Which crowdfunding model is most popular?

By far lender-based real estate crowdfunding is the most popular crowdfunding model. In 2014, 75.7 percent of all crowdfunding volume worldwide was lender-based and another 18.5 percent was equity based.

How much growth has there been in crowdfunding volume over the years?

Worldwide real estate crowdfunding volume increased from $396 million in 2013 to about $3.6 billion in 2016. That's a huge jump in four years. By 2025, real estate crowdfunding is expected to increase to $300 billion.[4] That's the true definition of explosive growth!

How many crowdfunding platforms are there?

In 2014, there were eighty-five crowdfunding platforms globally. In 2017, that number was expected to increase to over 2,000.[5]

These are some of the basic facts about real estate crowdfunding. I believe it is here to stay, that it is not a fad, and that it truly has the opportunity to be a disruptive force in real estate. If true, then how do we take advantage of this new technology and, at the same time, avoid being a lemming? The short answer is, do your homework. Here's how to do this:

- ✓ **Choose your crowdfunding platform wisely.** Not all platforms are equally good. Find out if they are well capitalized. Do they have qualified people at the top? Or are they led by two recent college graduates with no real estate experience?
- ✓ **Choose the crowdfunding model that works best for you.** I'm considering investing in a lender-based crowdfunding model. I think there is substantially less risk with this model (and likely a whole lot less reward) than the equity-based crowdfunding model. Of course, you need to decide what your best option would be.
- ✓ **Qualify your sponsor.** What is his track record? How much real estate experience does he have in senior management? Can you meet him?
- ✓ **What is the collateral of your investment?** Is it the real estate itself, or is it in an investment product structured by the crowdfunding company?

✓ **How leveraged is the investment?** Would it be over-leveraged if there were a downturn in the market?

✓ **How long is the proposed holding period?** Given the length, is that an acceptable time period? Currently there is no secondary market for crowdfunding investments, which means that the project will have to come to a completion before the investor can liquidate.

In the years ahead, it's quite possible that commercial real estate crowdfunding will expose an Achilles heel. But for now, I see it as a legitimate model for funding real estate. Proceed with caution, though. Do your homework. Start with modest-sized investments until you get a feel for what you're doing.

Whether you plan to invest on your own or with a proven real estate sponsor or through crowdfunding depends on how much time, money, and risk you want to invest. What's best for you is up to you.

If you plan to invest on your own or as the managing member of an LLC, the next chapter provides you with additional tips on how to do that successfully.

5

Selecting Your Advisory Team

Every person who invests in well-selected real estate in a growing section of a prosperous community adopts the surest and safest method of becoming independent, for real estate is the basis of wealth.
–Theodore Roosevelt, 26th president of the United States

If you've decided that you prefer investing on your own or with a small group of investors, my hat's off to you. It takes considerably more effort and a lot more risk doing it on your own. And with high risk comes the opportunity for high reward.

The next step is to choose your real estate advisory team. You can have as few as one—yourself. But a wise investor has a team of advisors. He realizes that his real estate experience is limited, and by adding experts in his areas of weakness, he helps reduce his risk of making poor investment decisions.

Your team could include one or more of the following:

> ➤ Real estate broker
> ➤ Commercial mortgage broker/loan officer
> ➤ Real estate attorney
> ➤ General contractor/building inspector
> ➤ Property manager

> ➤ Accountant

My suggestion is that you begin by asking real estate professionals you know and respect which people they can recommend. But don't stop there. Interview their recommendations as well.

THE FIVE UNASKED QUESTIONS

When interviewing prospective members of your real estate advisory team, make sure they answer the five unasked questions that will determine whether they get your business. You heard me right. There are five *unasked* questions that people universally want the answers to but won't ask because it would be considered impolite to ask. And yet, how well the interviewee does in answering these unasked questions will often determine whether you choose him or her for your team. Here they are:

1. Can I trust you? Are you looking out for my best interest or are you only in it for yourself?
2. Do you know what you're talking about—in other words, are you competent?
3. Do I like you?
4. How are you different from your competition?
5. If I do business with you, what's in it for me?

Can you imagine asking any of these questions directly to an interviewee? Not hardly. That would be rude. And yet, aren't these the questions you would like answered? So how can you go about finding answers to these questions?

Well, the best way to get answers to the first three questions about trust, competency, and likability is to have someone other than the one being interviewed answer them. Past clients are the best people to answer these three questions on the interviewee's behalf. This requires that you request references with telephone numbers. If interviewees are unwilling to provide references, then drop them like a hot potato. Their unwillingness is a big red flag that they shouldn't be added to your team. On the other hand, every time they give you the name and phone number of a satisfied client, it's confirmation that they're known for their quality work. And when one of their references responds positively with favorable comments, they are in essence saying about your prospective team member:

> ➢ You can trust him.
> ➢ He knows what he is talking about.
> ➢ I like him, and you will too.

The fourth question is about how well they differentiate themselves from their competition. For those of us who are commercial real estate professionals—whether we are involved in sales, leasing, lending, escrow and title work, legal, appraising, environmental, or what have you—we provide our clients a service, which is difficult in many instances to differentiate from our competitors. Let's be honest: for most of us, there are only nuance differences between our peers and us. But those real estate professionals who have been in the business a long time should be able to answer that fourth question unhesitatingly. If they can't differentiate their product or service from their competition, you need to find someone else to be on your team. On the other hand, I marvel at the loyalty of those real estate investors who will only use the services of one particular title company. How does a title company that provides near identical services with fixed prices generate such loyalty? Such companies do it by performing to a quality of service that exceeds the customer's expectations. And they do it consistently, over and over again.

The last question of the unasked questions is essentially, "What's in it for me?" There is a well-known saying that "No one likes to be sold, but everyone likes to buy." It's the responsibility of those you interview to articulate why it's in your best interest to hire their services. It certainly isn't for you to provide them with a paycheck.

Which of the five unasked questions is most important? I believe the most important is "Do I like you?" No one wants to do business with people who are annoying or self-centered. All things being equal, people would rather do business with people they enjoy being around. But ultimately, how well all five of these questions are answered will help you decide whom to choose for your real estate advisory team.

THE FOUR CLIENTS: WHICH ARE YOU?

In the book *Why I Left Goldman Sachs*, the author, Greg Smith, describes himself as "not very religious" but appreciative of the traditions around the Jewish holidays, especially the Passover Seder. He particularly likes the part of the story discussing the reaction of the Four Sons to Passover: one who is wise, one who is wicked, one who is simple, and one who doesn't know what questions to ask. He then goes on to say that just as in ancient Egypt it was told about the Four Sons, so too on Wall Street there are the Four Clients.

I believe that, just as there are Four Clients on Wall Street, there are also Four Clients in commercial real estate. These Four Clients represent universal truth. By that I mean it's as true today as it was three thousand years ago and as true as it will be three thousand years from now. And these Four Clients transcend all cultures that have ever existed or will exist.

The story of the Four Sons will help you identify whom you most closely resemble. And with that understanding, you will be able to better choose the type of advisory team members who can best work with your temperament. So read carefully and do an honest self-assessment.

1. Are You the Wise Client?

The wise ones are those I hope to always have as clients, and fortunately many of my clients fall into this category. They have excellent real estate experience. They know the ropes, but they also respect what I bring to the table. They realize I am an important cog in the wheel, and they don't grumble about the fee I earn.

My response: I treat them with the respect they deserve. I listen to them because I have the opportunity to learn from them. I bend over backwards to get the deal done as promised.

2. Are You the Wicked Client?

The Wicked Client knowingly withholds adverse information from me about the property or about himself in order to get the best possible outcome for himself. He has no problem cutting ethical corners if that is what it takes. He hopes that whatever he is hiding will stay hidden just long enough to get the deal done.

My response: When I find out that important information has been withheld, I disclose it to the light of day. To not disclose it makes me a party to his deception. So if it means I lose the transaction or the client, I do what is necessary so I can go to bed at night with a clear conscience.

3. Are You the Simple Client?

The Simple Client thinks he knows more about real estate than he actually does. He generally has an overinflated ego and, as a rule, does not trust anyone's judgment but his own. If left to his own ways, the outcome of the transaction will get done, but it will likely be a more painful process and have a less favorable outcome than if he would have taken my experienced counsel.

My response: It is my duty to protect the Simple Client from himself. I vigorously give him my best counsel and leave the decision making to him. As easy as it would be to be a yes-man, I don't capitulate to that. I provide sound direction, and even if he doesn't take it, he will, deep down, grudgingly admire that I wasn't his sycophant.

4. Are You the Client Who Doesn't Know What Questions to Ask?

These clients are the most vulnerable, the easiest to take advantage of. They are the ones who really shouldn't own real estate. After all, they don't even know what questions to ask, much less what else to do.

Recently I had a client who fell into this group. Her husband liked owning and managing real estate. He was an active investor. She, on the other hand, was a passive investor, allowing her husband to make all the real estate decisions. When he passed away, she found herself in a position where she had to make all the decisions on her own. This was strange and uninviting territory for her.

My response: I see it as my duty to guide such clients through the commercial real estate process. I give them wise counsel and charge them a fair fee for the services rendered. One definition of integrity is doing the right thing when no one is looking. With vulnerable clients, I show integrity when I treat them right, especially when they wouldn't realize if I were taking advantage of them.

So, which client are you? In reality, most of my clients are a combination of two or more of these traits. Do an honest self-assessment, and once you can honestly admit to yourself who you are, then find the real estate advisors who will work best with your personality bent. If you have a tendency under stress to cut ethical corners, find someone who will keep you on the straight and narrow. If you have a tendency to be a bit blustery, don't hire a yes-man. And if you believe you're in over your head, find the advisor who you believe will always be looking out for your best interest and not her own.

FOUR TYPES OF MORTGAGE BROKERS TO AVOID

As a commercial mortgage broker, I have a confession to get off my chest: It embarrasses me deeply to admit that mortgage brokers on the whole have a reputation equal to or possibly worse than used car salespersons. Unfortunately, in many instances, this poor reputation is well deserved. There are a lot of commercial mortgage brokers, for one reason or another, who don't care that they are sullying the reputation of their peers. I'm glad to say, though, that for every deadbeat commercial mortgage broker, there are several who are honest and professional in their behavior. But for those others, I have grouped them into four types of mortgage brokers—each of which you should avoid like the plague.

1. The Unqualified

Simply put, residential commercial mortgage brokers are totally unqualified to perform the duties necessary to represent a borrower's best interest for financing an income-producing property. They don't know:

- which lenders have the best rates and terms;
- how to identify issues that will potentially cause lenders to decline quoting on this deal;
- how to identify the mitigating factors that will help overcome these issues; or

➢ how to put together a preliminary loan package that would interest a lender in providing a letter of interest.

They are completely out of their league! Don't even think about using their services.

2. The Lazy

The lazy mortgage broker is the one who will not work hard to find financing for a deal that may be difficult to finance. You see, he doesn't want to put much effort into a deal that may require more time and work than he is willing to exert. Instead, he performs a quick analysis of the loan request on the back of a napkin and then calls his favorite lender. If the lender says yes, the lazy mortgage broker gets a letter of interest from him and his job is done. It doesn't matter to him if his favorite lender doesn't have the best rates and terms for this particular loan request. He certainly won't go elsewhere because that would require more effort than he wants to put in. And he certainly won't lift a finger to help the lender with loan processing. No, he will be totally passive, waiting until the appropriate moment to get his demand into escrow so he gets paid.

3. The Unprincipled

Some lenders, to encourage receiving more loan business from commercial mortgage brokers, will pay them a loan fee outside of loan closing. This fee from the lender to the broker will not show up on the closing statement. So instead of just receiving his customary fee from the borrower for services rendered, the unprincipled commercial mortgage broker will also receive a fee from the lender as well. Or even worse, a lender will ask if a commercial mortgage broker would like to "build a loan fee" into the loan spread. If he says yes, the borrower is unknowingly paying for the commercial mortgage broker's fee with a higher interest rate.

This practice may be unethical, but it's not against the law for a commercial mortgage broker to fail to disclose to his client that he is also receiving a fee from the lender. Unprincipled commercial mortgage brokers leave this uncomfortable little tidbit out of any conversation they have with their clients.

4. The Incompetent

Incompetency in the mortgage business takes many forms. It begins by not interviewing the client to find out specifically what he wants in a loan. In all honesty, the interview process is more of an art form than a science. Many borrowers really don't understand what they are looking for in a loan until you provide them with several options for comparison. Incompetency also rears its ugly head when the incompetent mortgage broker does not understand either the nuances of the transaction that can kill the deal or the mitigating circumstances that will save it. On the other hand, an unprincipled commercial mortgage broker may be aware of the "killer issue" but will try to hide any adverse information from the lender, hoping that he won't discover it until it's too late. A good commercial mortgage broker will disclose up front the "hair on the deal" that will cause lenders heartburn and then propose solutions to resolve these issues.

Another example of incompetency or being unprincipled (I'm not sure which) is when a commercial mortgage broker doesn't disclose all of the shortcomings of a particular loan alternative. For example, many borrowers have been blindsided by the consequences of having a loan with a yield maintenance prepayment penalty. The commercial mortgage broker should have told him in no uncertain terms what he was getting himself into if he proceeded with this type of prepayment penalty. Now, for some borrowers, a yield maintenance penalty is acceptable because they plan to keep the property forever. In their minds, the lower interest rate and possibly a longer amortization that comes with yield maintenance are worth it to them. But I wish I had a dollar for every time I met a borrower who regretted the day he financed his property with a loan that had a yield maintenance prepayment penalty. The property owner wants to either sell or refinance his property, but he can't because the prepayment penalty on his existing loan is "ginormous." If he had been told up front the consequences of having a yield maintenance prepayment penalty, he would never have proceeded with this loan alternative.

THE GOOD ONES

So now that I've scared you from ever using a commercial mortgage broker, let me assure you there are many hard working, principled, and competent commercial mortgage brokers in the business. A good one will:

➢ Optimize the rate and loan terms for their client's specific needs. They will shop the market and not focus on one or two of their favorite lending sources.

➢ Guide the client through the loan process, not just hand him off to the lender. They will proactively represent the client's best interest to the lender.

➢ Disclose all fees received from the lender outside of loan closing.

➢ Communicate with the client on a regular basis throughout the loan process, especially when adverse developments occur.

➢ Focus on the client's agenda and not their own, even if it is to their own detriment. If they are not able to add value, they will refer the client to someone who can.

When it comes to choosing a commercial mortgage broker, choose wisely.

6

An Introduction to the Numbers of CRE Investing

Ninety percent of all millionaires become so through owning real estate.
–Andrew Carnegie, industrialist, philanthropist

To be an expert commercial real estate investor requires having a solid grasp of the numbers associated with real estate investing. There are at least six different types of CRE calculations an investor needs to fully understand. Commonly, I find that investors are very knowledgeable in two or more of these categories but rarely all six.

1. How is commercial real estate valued?
2. How do you determine the loan amount based on a lender's underwriting parameters?
3. How do you calculate a property's cash-on-cash return?
4. How does leverage impact a property's cash-on-cash return?
5. How does loan amortization impact your investment?
6. What minimum financial requirements do lenders require of borrowers in order for them to be approved for a loan?

The subjects these questions focus on are the financial basics that all investors should know backwards and forwards. What follows are ten questions that introduce these types of real estate calculations.

How Knowledgeable a CRE Investor Are You? Take the Quiz and Find Out

HOW COMMERCIAL REAL ESTATE IS VALUED

1. When the capitalization rate goes down, the value of the property does what?
   A. Goes down
   B. Goes up
   C. The capitalization rate has no bearing on value
   D. Not enough information provided to make this determination

Use the following information for the next two questions:
   ➢ $5,000,000 purchase price
   ➢ 70 percent maximum loan-to-value Ratio (LTV)
   ➢ 1.25 minimum debt service coverage ratio (DSCR)
   ➢ 4.0 percent interest rate
   ➢ 25-year amortization
   ➢ $325,000 (NOI)

2. What is the capitalization rate for the property?
   A. 4.8 percent
   B. 5.5 percent
   C. 6.5 percent
   D. 7.1 percent

HOW THE LOAN AMOUNT IS CALCULATED

3. Based on the underwriting criteria of a maximum 70 percent LTV and a minimum 1.25 DSCR, what is the maximum loan amount (rounded to the nearest $100,000) the property can achieve?

A. $3,000,000
B. $3,200,000
C. $3,500,000
D. $4,100,000

HOW TO CALCULATE A PROPERTY'S CASH-ON-CASH RETURN

Use the following information to answer the next question:

➤ $5,000,000 purchase price
➤ $3,500,000 loan amount
➤ $325,000 net operating income (NOI)
➤ $221,691 annual mortgage payments

4. What is this property's cash-on-cash return?
   A. 4.2 percent
   B. 5.8 percent
   C. 6.9 percent
   D. 7.1 percent

HOW LEVERAGE AFFECTS A PROPERTY'S CASH-ON-CASH RETURN

5. Lowering the interest rate or lengthening the amortization improves the property's cash-on-cash return because, in both examples, the mortgage payment is reduced. What does increasing the loan amount do to the property's cash-on-cash return?
   A. It increases the cash-on-cash return
   B. It decreases the cash-on-cash return
   C. It has no impact on the cash-on-cash return
   D. Not enough information to make a determination

HOW AMORTIZATION AFFECTS YOUR REAL ESTATE INVESTMENT

6. Which amortization method will pay down the loan the fastest?

    A. Interest only

    B. 30/360

    C. Actual/360

    D. Not enough information provided to make a determination

7. Which amortization method will have the most positive influence on a property's cash-on-cash return?

    A. Interest only

    B. 30/360

    C. Actual/360

    D. Not enough information provided to make a determination

8. Which amortization method will the borrower pay more interest on over the life of the loan?

    A. Interest only

    B. 30/360

    C. Actual/360

    D. Not enough information provided to make a determination

MINIMUM FINANCIAL REQUIREMENTS LENDERS REQUIRE OF BORROWERS

9. As a rule of thumb, what is the minimum net worth that a borrower needs to qualify for a loan?

    A. 1 times the loan amount

    B. 2 times the loan amount

    C. 5 times the loan amount

    D. There is no rule of thumb requiring the borrower to have a particular net worth in relation to the loan size

10. As a rule of thumb, what is the absolute minimum amount of liquid assets a borrower must show on his personal financial statement in order to qualify for a loan?

    A. 6 months of mortgage payments on the property

    B. 9 months of mortgage payments on the property

    C. 10 percent of the loan amount

    D. All of the above

To find out how well you did on the quiz, go to the back of the book to Appendix 1 for the answer key. So how well did you do? Check yourself against the following table of results.

How **knowledgeable** a CRE investor are you?

Correct Answers	Type of Investor
8 - 10	Expert
6 - 7	Seasoned
4 - 5	Competent
0 - 3	Novice

Don't feel badly if you did poorly. Less than 10 percent of those who've taken the quiz are identified as expert investors. The average quiz score is four. If you didn't do well, find an online commercial real estate course that teaches the fundamentals of CRE investing. Knowing how to correctly do these calculations is critical to your success as a CRE investor.

A More Objective Approach to
Valuing Commercial Real Estate

Once you have a working knowledge of the most important CRE calculations, the next step is to find the right property to buy. This will likely require "kicking the tires" of several properties before the right one comes along.

Once you've focused your interest on a particular property, determining a price to offer is the next step. How do you go about determining what the property is worth? Making a realistic offer on a property is becoming more of an art form these days than an objective measurement. Here's why.

The Traditional Approach

Years ago, Tennessee Ernie Ford liked to say to the people he met, "Bless your pea-pickin' heart." I'm not sure what the phrase meant then or what it means now, but I'm reminded of the saying when I receive a marketing flyer for a new for-sale listing. It's full of pretty pictures of the property and nice sounding words of the neighborhood. And the most intriguing thing about many marketing flyers is the projected rents and expenses, which are in no way connected to reality. I can't help but think to myself, *Bless their pea-pickin' hearts. They must think I've fallen off the turnip truck!*

I've come to the realization that real estate brokers can't help themselves. They really can't. In order to be a real estate broker, you have to be a cockeyed optimist. There are too many down times in real estate, and in order for brokers to survive, they have to be "glass half full" type of people. I get that. But do they really think they are fooling anyone with the pie-in-the-sky income and expense projections they conjure up on their marketing flyers?

My Approach

My purpose in this section is not to skewer real estate brokers but to give you another approach for valuing a property which I believe is more objective. It begins by throwing away the meaningless marketing flyer and evaluating the property from three totally different perspectives.

Historical Perspective

Spread out the historical operating statements (preferably two full years plus year-to-date numbers) and the most recent rent roll to find out what's been going on at the property. How has it performed? Ask the seller to explain the abnormalities in the numbers. Find out the good, the bad, and the downright ugly.

Lender's Perspective

Once you have an understanding of the real income and expenses, put your lender's hat on and project how a lender will underwrite the property (the criteria lenders use to underwrite a property are explained below). Why should you care? Because the lender—not you or the real estate broker—will be the one who will size the loan. So you need to know how a lender will look at the property.

Buyer's Perspective

Once you understand the property's historical performance and the lender's perspective, let your creative juices flow. What ideas can you bring to this property that will make its performance zing—something that the current owner is totally clueless about?

If you want to try out my approach to valuing real estate, I've created a six-page Excel spreadsheet to facilitate the process. And the price is right. It's free. Go to my website, www.marshallcf.com. Go to Tools on the navigation bar at the top of the home page. On the drop-down menu, click on Property Investing Analysis Spreadsheet. Follow the instructions from there. This CRE investing spreadsheet will calculate the following:

> ➤ The estimated cap rate you're actually buying the property for based on *your* projection of income and expenses, not on the seller's or the appraiser's.
> ➤ How the lender will most likely size the loan based on his normal rules of thumb. Applying these rules typically lowers the projected cash flow before debt service, which results in a lower loan amount.
> ➤ The monthly mortgage payment for each lending alternative.

> ➢ An estimate of how much cash or 1031 exchange equity will be required by the buyer at closing in order to cover the down payment and all closing costs.
> ➢ And most importantly, the spreadsheet will calculate a before- and after-tax return on equity for each lending alternative considered.

Get my free CRE investing spreadsheet, or if you like, you can continue using the selling agent's marketing flyers. Bless their pea-pickin' hearts.

SEVEN RULES OF THUMB LENDERS USE TO SIZE YOUR LOAN

One of the more common mistakes of investing in real estate is not fully understanding the importance the lender has on a property's return on investment. Now you may be thinking: *Doug, of course the lender is important to a property's ROI. The lower the interest rate, the higher the ROI. Duh.* Yes, that's true, but that's not what I'm referring to.

Maybe even more critical to a property's return on investment is the size of the loan. It's the lender who ultimately determines this. Not the pro forma found in the marketing flyer or the buyer's proposed budget. It's the lender. And without having an accurate estimate of the loan amount, the buyer doesn't know how much cash is required at closing. And how much equity that's required to purchase the property is a key factor in determining the property's cash-on-cash return.

This is not an academic exercise. As an investor, the sizing of the loan is a critical component for calculating the property's return on investment. That's why it's important to understand that lenders have rules of thumb they use in their underwriting guidelines. Their guidelines have the potential of significantly affecting the property's cash-on-cash return. Not all lenders have the same underwriting rules. That would be too easy. Each lender sizes the loan differently, but generally there are seven rules of thumb that most lenders use to determine the loan amount. As capitalization rates decline, loan sizes are increasingly constrained by the lender's debt coverage ratio instead of their loan-to-value ratio. This puts additional importance on understanding these lender rules of thumb.

1. Annual Rental Income – Lenders, in most instances, use the current monthly gross potential rent (with vacant units at market) times twelve months. With sharply increasing rents, many investors and CRE professionals like to use current asking rents, also called turnover rents. Their reasoning is that current market rents have been proven, and as soon as the other tenants' leases expire, they will increase the rents to market. That may make sense from the buyer's point of view, but lenders generally only use the gross potential rent found on the most current rent roll.

2. The Vacancy Rate – This is determined by taking the lower of (a) the actual vacancy at the property, (b) the current vacancy rate in the market for that property type, or (c) 5 percent. With tight vacancy rates, especially in apartments and industrial properties, investors like to use a vacancy rate less than 5 percent. That might not make perfect sense, but lenders are not known for common sense. They are a conservative lot, so the best vacancy rate they will use is 5 percent.

3. Other Income – This is limited to those types of income that are easily quantifiable. For apartments that would mean garage income, storage income, laundry income, and utility reimbursements. For other property types, common area reimbursements (CAMs) would fall into this category. But income from late charges, application fees, pet rent, damage reimbursements, and the like will not be used.

4. Most Operating Expenses – Here I'm thinking of property taxes, insurance, utilities, and the like. These are increased 3 percent over the previous year. There are exceptions to this rule of thumb, specifically with repairs and maintenance, on-site payroll, and off-site management expenses, as I show below.

5. Repairs and Maintenance – For apartments, this would include turnover expenses and landscape maintenance. These types of expenses can vary greatly from one year to the next. Lenders will do one of two things with these: (a) they will average the past two or three years, or (b) they will defer to what's found in the appraisal. Depending on the age and size of the property, I generally use $500 per unit for repairs and maintenance,

$200 per unit for turnover expenses, and $300 per unit for landscape maintenance. For other property types, I use an historical average for repairs and maintenance.

6. On-Site Payroll and Off-Site Management Expenses – For apartments, most lenders will use as a rule of thumb between 10 to 12 percent of effective gross income for these two expense categories. For other property types, lenders will follow what's shown on the property's historical operating statements.

7. Capital Expenditures – For apartments, lenders will use no less than $250 per unit. If the property is older or has significant deferred maintenance, the cost per unit could go much higher. For other property types, it's anybody's guess what they'll use. Surprisingly, many lenders will not include any capital expenditures in their projection of expenses, which makes no sense to me.

Do Your Homework: Think Like a Lender

Adjusting the property's income and expenses with these seven rules of thumb has the potential of significantly decreasing the property's projected cash flow before debt service. As an investor, you need to think like a lender when it comes to sizing the loan. To avoid being unpleasantly surprised when you get your lender quotes, go through the exercise of applying these rules of thumb to your pro forma. At the very least, ask each lender how he or she will underwrite the loan. What are their specific rules of thumb for sizing the loan?

With that information in hand, ask yourself whether the lower loan amount that a typical lender will offer will kill the deal:

➢ Will it require more equity than you want to invest in the property?
➢ Or will the additional equity in the property reduce your cash-on-cash return below a level you find acceptable?

If either is the case, isn't it better to find this out early on in the buying process? Wouldn't you rather know this important piece of the investing puzzle prior to getting the property under contract?

Thinking like a lender will help you avoid wasting time and energy on a property that no longer pencils because the loan is lower than you hoped to receive.

WHY IRR IS A FOOL'S APPROACH TO VALUING COMMERCIAL REAL ESTATE

During my thirty-plus years in commercial real estate, I've realized that most savvy investors have their own unique method of valuing a property. And in most instances, the really successful real estate investors have a fairly simple analysis, an almost "back of the napkin" approach to making purchase decisions. It works well for them. They value properties based on a combination of a big picture (thirty-thousand-foot view of the property) and gut instinct.

Then there are a few investors I've worked with who like to "get in the weeds." They enjoy the process of getting as much data as possible to make an informed decision. This is my personality bent too. I want to make sure I'm not missing some arcane but important detail that will make my purchase decision a no-brainer. Where I differ from most of my fellow detail-oriented investors is on the best approach to analyzing a property. As a CCIM designee, I have been trained in Internal Rates of Return (IRR) and Net Present Value (NPV) valuation methods. But over time, I realized that approach assumes way too many variables you have no answer to when you purchase a property, such as:

> ➤ How much are rents going to increase over time?
> ➤ How long will you hold the property?
> ➤ What will be the rate of inflation over the holding period?
> ➤ What will be the cap rate at the time you sell the property?

The answers to these questions are unknowable. And yet what they ask us to project has to be done in order to determine an IRR. It's a classic example of GIGO (garbage in, garbage out). I've listened to CCIM instructors tell their students that you should buy the property with the highest IRR when one property had a 14.19 percent IRR and the other had a 14.23 percent IRR. Really?

Though I enjoy gathering and analyzing as many details as possible, my approach is much simpler than doing an IRR calculation. My property valuation method is based on knowable assumptions or at least reasonably educated guesses, such as:

> ➤ What will I offer for the property in an as-is condition?
> ➤ What is needed to renovate the property, and how much will it cost?
> ➤ When the improvements are completed, what will be the new market rents?
> ➤ How long will it take me to achieve stabilized occupancy?
> ➤ What type of financing should I get? A permanent loan with a holdback for repairs? Or a full-blown bridge loan followed by a competitive nonrecourse loan?

All of these questions require and can receive at the very least educated guesses. Once these questions are answered objectively as possible with the most likely outcomes, they can be inputted into a CRE investing spreadsheet. I focus in on a before-tax return-on-equity in the first year of stabilized operation. If it's in the 5 percent or better range, then I know the property will do well over time.

Now you may be thinking, *This guy is just intimidated by the sophistication of the IRR method.* Not so. I actually enjoy doing an IRR calculation. It's so analytical, and I love that. I just don't believe it provides the best approach to making a buy/no-buy decision. It reminds me of the Mark Twain saying, "There are liars, damned liars, and then there are statisticians." Here are two examples of what I mean:

> ➤ Depending on your assumptions, you can get whatever IRR you want to get. If your IRR is not high enough to justify purchasing the property, then increase your annual rent growth by 1 percent or lower your sales cap rate in year ten by fifty basis points. Thirty years ago, as a financial analyst for a syndicator, that was my job. I played with the numbers until I got the desired return my boss wanted for our investor presentations.

➢ In my opinion, cash flow is king. But you can use an IRR calculation to justify purchasing a property having little or no annual cash flow. You can also use it to achieve a higher IRR by inflating the sales price in year ten over a property that has generous cash flows over the holding period. I would rather choose the property with the good cash flow and slightly lower IRR than the property with little cash flow and higher IRR. Wouldn't you?

Now that the IRR aficionados have labeled me an IRR Neanderthal, I must confess that I do use a before-tax IRR calculation *after* I've sold a property. At that point, all the variables are known. I know:

➢ how much equity was required when I purchased the property;
➢ my annual owner distributions;
➢ the number of years I owned the property; and
➢ the amount of cash or 1031 equity I received at closing when I sold the property.

Knowing those four things, I can then run an accurate IRR calculation.

The properties I've sold have had an IRR as low as 7 percent and as high as 28 percent. But I calculate an IRR calculation *after* the property is sold, not *before*. Doing so after the property is sold yields an informed and accurate return on my investment. In contrast, using the IRR method to value a potential purchase is a fool's approach to valuing commercial real estate because there are too many unknown variables.

If you would like to learn the specifics of how I analyze a property purchase, I would encourage you to listen to a short two-minute video presentation on my website at http://marshallcf.com/spread-sheet/ and then download for free my Property Investing Analysis Spreadsheet.

7

How to Successfully Close
on Your CRE Purchase

*Successful investing takes time, discipline and patience. No
matter how great the talent or effort, some things just take
time: You can't produce a baby in one month by getting
nine women pregnant.*
–Warren Buffett, billionaire investor

At this point in the buying process you've identified a property you're interested in making an offer on. And because you now have a working knowledge of the most important CRE calculations, you know how much you believe the property to be worth. The next step in the process is for your real estate broker to formalize an offer for the property that is agreeable to you, the buyer, and the seller. An experienced real estate broker knows how to negotiate an acceptable price for the property as well as other terms on the Purchase and Sale Agreement.

POTENTIAL TRAPS TO NEGOTIATE AWAY
ON THE PURCHASE AND SALE AGREEMENT

Have you ever wondered when signing a boilerplate Purchase and Sale Agreement (PSA) what paragraphs have the potential to come back and haunt you before the sale is complete? Here are four potential issues that buyers should do their best to negotiate away before they sign the PSA.[6]

Avoid Calling Earnest Money Non-Refundable

Define the terminology correctly. "Hard" or "non-refundable" is not technically correct because, in certain situations, the earnest money deposit is refundable. The earnest money still remains refundable if the seller fails to perform his or her obligations, the property is condemned, or there is a failure of a specific closing condition.

Unacceptable Title Exceptions

As soon as possible, carefully review all exception documents in the preliminary title report, including Covenants, Conditions, and Restrictions (CC&R) and easements. Have the right to terminate the PSA if there are title exceptions that are unacceptable to the buyer.

Notices to Seller Identified in the Purchase and Sale Agreement

In a rising real estate market, sellers may want to find any excuse possible to cancel the PSA because a higher sales price has been subsequently received since it was signed. To avoid this from occurring, buyers need to make sure all deadlines on the PSA are explicitly stated with no wiggle room for misunderstanding between both parties. The buyer then needs to comply with the specified deadlines for notifying the seller of compliance with the PSA's terms. Avoid missing any deadlines so that the seller cannot use a missed deadline as a pretext to cancel the PSA.

Unreasonably Short Financing Period

This is one of my pet peeves because it affects me, the commercial mortgage broker. I am always baffled why a buyer would agree to remove the financing contingency within forty-five days or less of signing the PSA. The reason a buyer uses a commercial mortgage broker is to get the best possible financing for the property. This requires shopping the market. A preliminary loan package cannot be sent to lenders until the seller releases the historical operating statements and current rent roll. The release of these documents usually occurs a couple of days after both parties sign the PSA.

So the earliest a loan package can be sent to prospective lenders is three days after signing the PSA. It takes about seven to ten days for lenders to respond with a letter of interest. The buyer then chooses a lender and signs their term sheet or what's known in the business as a letter of interest. It generally takes forty-five to fifty days from signing the LOI to receiving loan approval. It takes another ten to fifteen days to close. Adding up all the days to get to loan approval requires a minimum of fifty-five days and then sixty-five days to close. It can even take an extra week, ten days, and more.

If the buyer must accept an unreasonably short financing period or lose the deal, make sure to negotiate extensions with a reasonable increase in earnest money.

How Real Estate Brokers Can Help Close Your Deal

Once you get a property under contract, it is imperative that your CRE advisory team does everything they can to get the transaction closed. You certainly don't want one of your team members to be the cause of a sales transaction going sideways, and yet many times they can inadvertently put a deal at risk.

Shown below are eight ways real estate brokers can help your chances of closing on your deal.[7]

1. Listing brokers use *realistic* pro forma numbers in your marketing packages. Good, solid numbers that can be supported by the historical operating statements make everyone's job (buyer, broker, appraiser, commercial mortgage broker, and lender) that much easier.

2. Listing brokers accept the responsibility of getting property documentation from the seller into a format acceptable to the buyer. Without good property documentation, the decision to buy is put at risk. The goal should be to make it as easy as possible for the buyer to agree to buy the property. Once the buyer accepts the deal, the property documentation used to get the buyer to say yes helps the appraiser and lender do their jobs too.

3. The buyer's broker gets involved in assisting the client with choosing the commercial mortgage broker/lender. As a broker, you are perceived as knowledgeable when you can recommend a competent commercial mortgage broker to assist your client. It also increases your probability of getting paid.

4. The buyer's broker communicates regularly with the other real estate professionals (the commercial mortgage broker, lender, escrow officer, appraiser, and so on) who are working to close the transaction. We are all on the same team. The buyer's broker should consider himself the quarterback leading his team to the finish line.

5. Real estate brokers use *realistic* deadlines in the sales agreement. A good commercial mortgage broker can assist you in determining reasonable timelines for when the loan will be approved and when it will close.

6. Real estate brokers are proactive about the issues, not reactive. A good real estate broker anticipates what the issues are going to be and then presents his rationale with sound documentation that mitigates these issues.

7. The buyer's broker encourages the borrower to get her personal loan documentation in to the lender quickly, thoroughly, and accurately. Again, the goal should be to make the loan process as easy as possible so that the lender can get it approved.

8. Don't violate the Golden Rule of lending, which is "He who has the gold makes the rules." Accept that the lender has a process he must follow. Your job is to help the commercial mortgage broker/lender get the loan approved so the deal gets done in a timely manner.

When your team of advisors works together with the buyer's broker acting as the quarterback, it's a beautiful thing to watch. Communication between team members occurs regularly. Each member understands and appreciates the importance of the other members' roles in the process. Everyone understands that the goal is to get the property purchased with as few hiccups in the process as possible. And when the deal finally closes, it's a cause for celebration and high fives among all team members.

Part 2

Financing Commercial Real Estate

8

How to Get the Best Possible Loan for Your Property

Don't stretch yourself too much with a mortgage. Buy within your means … it's not worth the sleepless nights.
–Sarah Beeny, developer and television host

How do you go about getting the best possible loan for your property? You should know the answer to this question.

Getting the best possible loan for your property is like completing a challenging crossword puzzle. The words going across the page and the words going down the page have to mesh perfectly together in order to complete the puzzle. The same is true for getting the best loan on your property. All the financing steps in the process need to come together perfectly in order to ensure an optimal outcome. Getting good rates and terms truly isn't rocket science. It's mostly common sense. But surprisingly few people understand how to go about it.

OPTIONS FOR FINANCING: HOW INVOLVED DO YOU WANT TO BE?

When shopping for a mortgage loan, you have three basic options. Which one you choose depends on the advantages and disadvantages important to you. You can:

1. Finance your property with a lender you have already done business with.
2. Shop the mortgage market on your own.
3. Employ the services of a commercial mortgage broker to shop the market for you.

For most property owners, the option that significantly improves their chances of getting the best possible loan for their property is option 3—using the services of a commercial mortgage broker. Later I'll explain why this is true. In the meantime, if you decide to find financing on your own, I'll tell you how to improve your chances of getting a better loan than what you would have obtained on your own. This requires applying several common sense principles that I've learned the hard way over the years. I want you to know these principles so you will have an easier time securing the financing you need if you decide to shop the mortgage market on your own. Still, I want to emphasize that, in most instances, using a commercial mortgage broker will improve your chances even more. I invite you to draw your own conclusions as I outline the do's and don'ts of each of the three options.

9

Option 1: Use a Lender You've Already Done Business With

We at Chrysler borrow money the old-fashioned way.
We pay it back.
–Lee Iacocca

When I talk to real estate owners about financing, it's not uncommon for them to say to me something like, "I take all my banking needs to my favorite lender." Generally there are two reasons for their response. First, it could be that I haven't gained their trust, so their response is just an easy way to get rid of me. If that's the case, then I got what I deserved. You don't ask for someone's business until you have their trust. Second, they may actually believe what they say. They really think their favorite lender is serving them well. Now if that's what they think, then I try my hardest not to say out loud, "Are you really that foolish?"

So let me ask you: Is convenience or loyalty so important to you that you would accept a less competitive loan with your existing lender than what a commercial mortgage broker can find for you? If a commercial mortgage broker can save you $50,000 in interest expense, net of his loan fee, over the life of the loan, why wouldn't you take it? Perhaps you don't want to take the time to gather the appropriate documents for a commercial mortgage broker so a lender can give you a quote. How long would that take you? Maybe a couple of hours? Is not being inconvenienced more important to you than saving $50,000? You

74

would be surprised how often a borrower would rather stay with their existing lender because to check out what's available in the market may inconvenience them a few hours in gathering the required information.

Let's back up for a moment. Financing your property with your current lender assumes three things that may or may not be true. It assumes that your favorite lender is still in business, that he's still lending, and that his rates and terms have not changed, at least not adversely. But in today's lending environment, your favorite lender of choice may no longer exist. If she is still around, she may not be lending. And if she is still lending, her rates and terms may not be as good as they once were.

But let's assume your favorite lender is still in the lending business. In that case, convenience is the primary advantage of financing your property with her. It certainly is the path of least resistance, and in most cases, it should be the quickest way to get the job done.

The disadvantage of this approach is that you'll never know whether you received the best rates and terms currently in the market. Think about it. What are the chances that your existing lender has the best financing available of all the potential lenders to choose from? That would be the equivalent of picking the proverbial needle out of a haystack. Not likely, is it? However, if convenience and ease of doing business are your top priorities in choosing a loan, you need go no further than back to a previous lender you've already done business with.

Personally, I don't see why anyone would go back to their existing lender without at least calling a commercial mortgage broker to get his or her opinion. A quick conversation over the phone with a good commercial mortgage broker should clarify for you how your existing lender's rate and terms compare to the market. Just say something like this to the commercial mortgage broker: "I don't want to waste your time so let me tell you the quote I've already received from my favorite lender and then you tell me whether that's competitive or not." Then tell him the proposed rate and terms. The commercial mortgage broker will appreciate that you realize his time is valuable, and he will likely know if the quote you have from your existing lender is competitive. If he thinks he can improve on your quote, he'll tell you. And if he knows that he can't, he'll tell you that too. He doesn't want to waste his time shopping the market if he already knows it's unlikely he can improve upon your quote.

If he tells you that he can land you a better deal, you're still not obligated to use his services. But if you want the best loan possible for your property, you owe it to yourself to shop the market. And if this is what you decide, you have another choice to make: Do you shop the market on your own (option 2), or do you use a commercial mortgage broker to do it for you (option 3)?

10

Option 2: Shop the Market on Your Own

Don't work for money; rather let money work for you.
Nobody can become really rich and stay wealthy by
working for money.
−www.geckoandfly.com

If you're going to shop the market without the services of a commercial mortgage broker, you need to do it the right way. So how do you go about contacting lenders for loan quotes? I have two important tips to improve your chances of getting the best loan possible: do your homework to find the most competitive lenders available, and be sure to sound like a professional over the phone. Let's discuss both of these in detail.

DO YOUR HOMEWORK

You have to do your homework to find the most competitive lenders. But how do you find them for your specific property type? Do you just Google lenders in your local area? Try it. See how that works. You'll find that it will get you nowhere. There are no shortcuts that you can take to find lenders with competitive financing. The process isn't easy, but it's critical that you take whatever time it takes to do a thorough search of the market to find the most competitive lenders.

I suggest you start by contacting other real estate professionals (real estate brokers, appraisers, escrow officers, and real estate attorneys) or, better yet, other owners of real estate who may be able to recommend their lenders to you. While this sounds like a good, sensible approach to finding the right lender, you'd be surprised how few people (even real estate professionals) know where to go for financing.

This step will take some time, so be persistent. Follow all the leads given, and if you're fortunate, you may discover that one or two lenders appear to be recommended more often than all the others. That's a clue that you may be on the right path.

SOUND PROFESSIONAL OVER THE PHONE

Make sure when you call potential lenders that you can succinctly explain your loan request. Here's a little secret: Loan officers can be abrasive over the phone and generally don't suffer fools gladly. But in fairness to them, you need to look at the conversation from their perspective. Understand that most loan officers are paid a very modest salary along with a commission based on loan volume. So to them, time is money. They receive hundreds of telephone calls a year, and they use the first sixty seconds of the call to determine whether it is worth their time to continue the conversation. If they don't know you, their inclination will be to get you off the phone as fast as possible with a quick no.

So you have to be prepared. You need to have the equivalent of an "elevator speech" prepared in advance that explains in bullet-point fashion why your loan proposal is perfect for them to finance. Get to the point quickly in a business-like manner with just the facts, such as:

> ➢ Property type
> ➢ Proposed loan amount
> ➢ Whether this is a refinance or an acquisition
> ➢ The property's net operating income
> ➢ Loan to value based on what you think is a reasonable cap rate
> ➢ The property's debt coverage ratio
> ➢ Your net worth, liquidity, and real estate experience

> ➤ Anything else that gives the loan officer a quick understanding of the loan proposal

And you better know how to talk his language—NOI, DCRs, LTVs, cap rates, to name just a few. If you don't come off professionally over the phone, the conversation will likely come to an abrupt end.

If you would like a quick primer on these terms and many others, go to my website: www.marshallcf.com. Click on the Resources tab at the top of the page and scroll down the drop down menu to Glossary of Real Estate Terms. There you'll see the definitions of most of the commonly used real estate and financing terms that'll make you sound like a pro.

So let's say you get the loan officer's attention in your opening pitch. You then go into further details of the deal. Be sure to tell him the "hair" that's on the deal. There's almost always some critical issue on every deal, especially in today's market. Your motto should be "disclose, disclose, disclose." It's better to get a quick no because you admitted the major issue up-front rather than surprising the lender later and losing all trust with him. And it's easier to sleep at night. If you're open with the loan officer, he should be able to tell you in the first couple of minutes whether or not he'll want to receive a loan package from you.

Provide a Professional-Looking Loan Package

The next step is to send a preliminary loan package to those lenders who expressed initial interest in financing your property.

What exactly is a lender looking for? To begin with, a lender wants you to answer the question, "Why would I want to put a loan on this property?" The loan package should answer that question as completely as possible.

Just as importantly, your loan package should exude professionalism. You would be shocked at how often loan officers receive a sloppy looking loan package that screams out to them, *I take no pride in my work, and I'm clueless as to what you're looking for in a good loan.* Consider: other than the initial phone call, no other source of communication speaks more clearly as to who you are than your preliminary loan package. If it comes across as poorly put together, what does that infer about you? The property and the loan request may be right down a lender's strike zone, but if it looks like you don't know what you're doing, you've significantly reduced your chances of gaining the lender's interest. Remember this vital piece of advice: Perception is often times more important than reality. You're asking a lender to lend you lots of money. You better have a package that tells him you're worth the risk. If you don't, you're wasting your time.

So what should a loan package include? At minimum, it should include the following documentation:

Property Information
> A one- or two-page executive summary summarizing the loan request
> A pro forma of income and expenses that can be justified by the historical operating statements
> Two full years, plus the current YTD, operating history on the property
> A current rent roll
> Photos of the property

Borrower Information
This would include all borrowers with managing control of the ownership entity or at least 20 percent or more interest in the property. This information would contain:

> A personal financial statement
> A real estate owned schedule
> Bank/brokerage statements (the two most recent ones) that verify the liquidity that is shown on the borrower's personal financial statement
> Two years of personal tax returns
> A brief résumé on the owner's real estate background

Provide a *complete* preliminary loan package or risk being considered a lightweight.

Once the loan officer has reviewed your package and hopefully expressed interest in your loan request, the lender should be willing to provide you with a letter of interest or, as it is called in the business, an LOI. Fight the urge to accept a loan quote over the phone. It's meaningless. Get the quote in writing. If he isn't willing to provide this, he isn't really interested. Move on to the next lender.

When you've received two or more written loan quotes, the fun begins.

HOW TO SIGNIFICANTLY IMPROVE YOUR LOAN QUOTES

If you negotiate well with your lenders, you may be able to significantly improve your rates and terms. You must do three things to improve your loan quotes.

The first step is to get the lenders competing against one another to get your business. Even in today's lending environment, if a lender knows she doesn't have the best quote on the table, she will often go back to her underwriter and see if the quote can be tweaked to make it more competitive. Yet, asking for an improvement on a loan quote should be done tactfully. If done in a heavy-handed manner, you will only irritate the lenders, which in all likelihood will backfire on you. So be very careful.

However, if you make the request tactfully, you may be pleasantly surprised by how much a lender can sweeten her proposal if she thinks she's going to lose the deal to one of her competitors. So it doesn't hurt to casually mention who she's competing against. Understand that the loan officer personally knows her competitors in most instances, and if she has any ounce of competitiveness flowing in her veins, she'll do what she can to win the business just for the pure satisfaction of winning a deal from one of her arch rivals.

Second, negotiate *before* signing the loan application, not after. A critical mistake borrowers can make is trying to negotiate an important issue *after* they've signed the loan application. Once you've signed the document, you've given up your negotiating power. The time to negotiate is *before* signing the application. At that point, you share negotiating power with the lender.

If you do a good job with this negotiation, the lender doesn't know whether she is going to lose the deal if she fails to comply with your request. Tell her that you're still deciding between her loan proposal and one of her competitors. Identify in your mind what is *the* critical issue that needs to be resolved favorably. That's what should be driving your negotiations. Then tell the loan officer that you would like to choose her loan proposal, but you have this one issue that needs to be resolved before you can sign the loan application. And don't get greedy. Stick with the key issue that needs improvement.

If you frame the discussion this way, the loan officer will do whatever she can to satisfy your issue because she is now emotionally more committed to getting this loan under application than you are. Or at least, that is what you want her to think. So if your negotiating point is within reasonable bounds of something that can be done, you're likely to get agreement in your favor.

The final thing you must do to get a better loan quote has nothing to do with negotiating with your lenders, but it has everything to do with wisely choosing which lender quote is the best for you. So don't focus too heavily on one loan parameter. That's really not a good approach for choosing a lender and here's why. A better approach is to review the pros and cons of each loan quote and then decide. For example, many borrowers' hot button is getting the lowest interest rate. But many times the lowest interest rate comes with an onerous yield maintenance prepayment penalty. Or maybe it comes with a shorter amortization that cuts deeply into the property's cash flow. Does the borrower still want the lowest rate then? Maybe not. In fact, it's not uncommon that when comparing the loan quotes in detail, the borrower chooses another lender rather than the one originally considered as the first choice.

HOW TO KEEP YOUR LOAN FROM GOING TO THE BOTTOM OF THE PILE

Carefully analyze all the pros and cons of each loan quote, and then decide which lender has the best rate and terms for you. Once you've decided which lender's LOI to choose, go ahead and sign the loan application and write the lender a check for the application deposit.

Congratulations! You've come a long way. But you're only halfway to the finish line: the loan still needs to close in a timely fashion and with the rate and terms shown on the letter of interest. In other words, it's one thing to get the loan application you wanted; now you've got to get it closed in the opportune time.

I have two very important tips that will significantly improve your chances of that happening. First of all, do not dribble the loan documentation to the lender. Once you have chosen your lender, make the loan process as easy as possible for her. Complete the lender's forms quickly, thoroughly, and accurately.

Most lender forms are, at best, poorly worded and many times inane. Accept that as being true and fill in every box on the form to the best of your ability, no matter how silly or irrelevant you find it. Your goal should be to complete all of the lender forms within the first two weeks of signing the loan application. You want everything thoroughly completed well before the appraisal is done so you don't cause a delay in the underwriting process.

A borrower who is unwilling to focus on getting the forms to the lender in a timely manner is putting his loan at risk by increasing the chances that the underwriter will cool to doing his loan. At best your loan closing will be unnecessarily delayed. If the lender doesn't have your documentation by the time the appraisal comes in, your deal will go directly to the bottom of her pile. At worst, depending on the length of the delay, it could kill your loan. I'm not exaggerating. The saying "Strike when the iron is hot" applies to lending. When the lender is emotionally in favor of your deal, make sure she has everything she needs so she can get you a quick approval.

The second thing you need to do in order to get the loan closed in a timely manner is not violate the golden rule of lending, which is "He who has the gold makes the rules." Each lending institution has its own unique way of underwriting, processing, and closing loans. Don't get into an argument about their process. To do so is futile. You will not win. All your arguing will do is create bad feelings, which is not what you want to do with those who have the ability to approve or decline your loan. Instead, provide them with what they are asking for in the manner they have requested it. You'll be better off in the end.

11

Option 3: Employ the Services of a Commercial Mortgage Broker

*Financial freedom is available to those
who learn about it and work for it.*
–Robert Kiyosaki, author of *Rich Dad, Poor Dad*

I believe using a commercial mortgage broker will optimize your chances of getting the best possible loan for your property.

There are four distinct advantages of using a commercial mortgage broker. The first is, *he knows more lending sources than you do.* Recall that the first step in shopping for a loan on your own is finding which lenders have the most competitive rates and loan terms. That is not an easy undertaking. The primary advantage of using a commercial mortgage broker is that he knows the lenders who have the most competitive rates and terms. Not all lenders are interested in your specific loan, but a broker likely knows those lenders who are. In fact, it's his job to know.

A good commercial mortgage broker regularly works with five to fifteen lenders, depending on who is the most competitive at the moment for a particular property type. Sometimes he knows that his most trusted lending sources do not have the rate and terms he needs to win the business. When that happens, a good broker has another ten or more lenders he has called on over the years who would be eager to do business with him again. He will find the most competitive loan terms because, if he doesn't, he will not get your business.

The second reason for using a commercial mortgage broker is that *he has already established a relationship based on trust with his lending sources.* This is one of the most overlooked advantages of employing his services. Developing trust between the borrower and the lender is essential for insuring a successful loan outcome. In commercial real estate, trust is everything. It is absolutely vital for getting a transaction completed.

If you've never worked with a particular lender, a trust relationship has not been established. On the other hand, a commercial mortgage broker may have worked on several loans with this lender. They know each other. They know each other's idiosyncrasies, and because of their prior relationship, there is a higher probability of getting the loan closed with a commercial mortgage broker than by you going directly to the same lender. That's right. You, the borrower, can go to the same lender and be turned down for a loan because you have no relationship with the lender. The commercial mortgage broker, on the other hand, has done several deals with this lender, and because they know and trust each other, the lender is willing to proceed with a loan application. As a borrower, why not take advantage of these established relationships between the commercial mortgage broker and the lender? Why not leverage those relationships?

Now some people will say that using a commercial mortgage broker will cost you an additional loan fee. That could happen, but it may not. It just depends on the lender. Let's assume for the moment that such a fee is charged to you. Many times, because the commercial mortgage broker knows where to go to get the best rates and terms, any additional fee is more than offset by a lower interest rate, a longer amortization, or more loan dollars than what you would have found shopping the mortgage market on your own. The old saying "Penny wise, pound foolish" applies here. You may save some money on the front end by not using the services of a commercial mortgage broker if he charges an additional loan fee. But you could easily pay out much more money on the back end without his expertise and relationships.

Third, compared to shopping the market on your own, *this option takes significantly less time and effort on the part of the owner.* Recall all of the steps you have to go through when shopping the market independently. There's a lot of work to do! But if you use a commercial mortgage broker, he will do the heavy lifting of finding the right lender and processing the loan. This will save you a great deal of time and effort.

The fourth and final reason for using a commercial mortgage broker is, *he can be your best advocate if things go wrong.* There are times in the loan process where you need someone to be your advocate, someone who strenuously defends your best interests. This can best be accomplished by a commercial mortgage broker who has an established relationship with the lender. The lender wants to keep the commercial mortgage broker happy because she doesn't want to jeopardize her relationship with him. He brings her deals, which is in her best interest. She wants him to continue bringing deals to her, so it's in her best interest to be fair to his clients or next time he may go to one of her competitors. Now compare the commercial mortgage broker's importance to the lender with *your* importance to the lender. In most instances, lenders will likely see you as a "one-off" transaction and won't consider the loss of your loan as having anywhere near the impact of losing a valued relationship with a commercial mortgage broker. Now consider the loan officer. Can the lender's loan officer adequately fill this role of advocate if something were to go wrong with the loan? She works for the lender. She is being paid by the lender. Whose best interest do you think she is looking after? Yours or the bank's? So the commercial mortgage broker is your best choice for advocate if things go wrong with your loan. Neither you nor the loan officer can fill that need nearly as well as the commercial mortgage broker can. A good commercial mortgage broker will "go nuclear" if the actions of the lender are so egregious that it requires drastic measures to handle what she's done.

Years ago, a lender approved a loan for one of my clients as proposed on the letter of interest. But prior to closing the loan, the lender changed their minds without notifying the borrower or me that they had reduced the amortization from twenty-five years down to fifteen years, effectively killing the property's cash flow. The reduced amortization was only revealed at closing. I told my client to walk out of the closing without signing anything. The borrower was distraught. I then wrote a letter to the loan officer's superior that included a copy of an email from the loan officer stating that the loan was approved with a twenty-five-year amortization. I went on to say in my letter that if the borrower decides to litigate this matter, I would be more than willing to testify on his behalf. In response, the lender decided to honor the original twenty-five-year amortization. And because I chose to go to bat for my client, I lost what had been a good lending relationship. But a good commercial mortgage broker does what he has to in order to protect his client.

These are the four reasons I believe you should use a commercial mortgage broker. Of course, the final decision is yours.

HOW TO CHOOSE A COMMERCIAL MORTGAGE BROKER

I'm going to let you in on a secret: not all commercial mortgage brokers are equally trustworthy, competent, and likeable. So if you've decided to use a commercial mortgage broker, then I have three very important suggestions to help you choose the right one.

First, when selecting a commercial mortgage broker, absolutely do not consider using a residential commercial mortgage broker. Residential mortgages and commercial real estate mortgages are completely different loan products. Residential mortgage brokers do not have the expertise to finance real estate loans. They will be totally out of their element, and they will completely mess it up.

Second, don't just choose a commercial mortgage broker. Interview several and then decide. They will be representing you, and you want the best qualified and most enjoyable person to help you through this process.

Where do you find commercial mortgage broker candidates to interview? Ask around. Specifically ask other property owners if they used a commercial mortgage broker that they could recommend. I also suggest that you contact other CRE professionals: real estate brokers, escrow officers, and attorneys, to name just a few. Prepare several questions ahead of time, including some of the following:

> ➢ What are your qualifications?
> ➢ How long have you been in business?
> ➢ How many lending sources do you generally work with?

> ➢ Can you give me the names and contact information for three property owners who have recently used your services?

Through the course of the interview determine, as best you can, whether you can trust this person, whether he is competent, and, maybe most importantly, whether he is likeable. Everything being equal, you would rather do business with someone you like, so determine whether the person fits this criterion.

Finish your interview with this question: "How are you different than your competition?" There are several ways commercial mortgage brokers can differentiate themselves from their competition, but I've got two ways that will help you "separate the sheep from the goats."

First, ask him or her, "How do you go about comparing loan quotes?" Good commercial mortgage brokers will provide their clients a side-by-side comparison of the lender quotes they receive. Lazy brokers won't do this because it requires more effort on their part than they'll want to put in. You don't want to hire lazy people. If you would like to see an example of a loan quote comparison that I've done for my clients, go to my website: www.marshallcf.com. Go to the top of the home page and click on Tools. Scroll down the drop down menu to Mortgage Solutions Blueprint and click on it. Scroll down the page to the Mortgage Solutions Blueprint Archive. To gain access, you need to provide your contact information. Once you're in, you will see several loan quote comparisons to choose from. Click on one, and you'll see how much easier it is to compare loan quotes when they're shown side by side.

A loan quote comparison will have at the top of the page the names of the lenders. Down the side of the page will be all the loan parameters a borrower needs to know in order to make an informed decision, such as loan amount, interest rate, loan term, amortization, loan fee, other financing costs, and type of prepayment penalty. Reviewing individual loan quotes can be confusing, so a side-by-side comparison displays the differences between each lender proposal, making it much easier for you decide which loan is best for you.

Ask each commercial mortgage broker to bring to the interview an example of what he provides his clients to compare loan quotes. If he does not show you some type of loan quote comparison spreadsheet, I would suggest you not choose him as your commercial mortgage broker. It's that important.

Second, ask interviewees whether they disclose to their client when they receive lender rebates. Many borrowers are unaware that some lenders pay rebates to commercial mortgage brokers outside of closing. And the vast majority of commercial mortgage brokers do not disclose to their clients that they're receiving these rebates. As a result, a borrower thinks he is being charged a 1 percent loan fee from the broker when, in fact, the lender is paying an additional fee to the commercial mortgage broker of a half a point or more outside of escrow. In order to do this, lenders will charge a higher interest rate to the borrower to compensate for the additional fee provided to the commercial mortgage broker. So you, the borrower, without your knowledge, may be paying for the undisclosed loan fee through a higher interest rate. You want someone who is above reproach in this area. Choose a commercial mortgage broker who discloses when and how much of a rebate he's receiving from his lending sources and whether the rebate is increasing your interest rate.

My last bit of advice to you is this: *Be loyal to the commercial mortgage broker you choose.* Once you've completed your interviews, choose one and only one commercial mortgage broker to represent you. Then be loyal to him by using him exclusively. If you do, it will work to your advantage and here's why. When a borrower uses the services of more than one commercial mortgage broker, without their knowledge, all trust between the borrower and the broker evaporates. That essential bond is destroyed. For example, let's say you've decided to use Commercial Mortgage Broker A. If he calls one of his lending sources and discovers that Commercial Mortgage Broker B has already talked to them about your loan request, do you think Broker A is going to work very hard getting you the best rates and terms possible? Not a chance. He'll feel betrayed and rightly so. And you will have undercut yourself in the process. Furthermore, when a lender receives telephone calls from different commercial mortgage brokers for the same property, it's a big turn-off. It signals to her that the property is being shopped to death. As a result, she loses interest and puts only a minimal effort into the loan quote. The best approach is to decide which commercial mortgage broker you want to represent you, and then stick with him to get the best rates and terms possible.

There you have it—my suggestions on choosing a commercial mortgage broker, the questions to ask potential mortgage brokers in the interview process, and how best to work with them once you've chosen who you want representing you.

DECISION TIME

Now you're ready to decide the final question. Which of the three options is best for you? Do you: (1) use a lender you've already done business with, (2) shop the market on your own, or (3) employ the services of a commercial mortgage broker? How you ultimately choose to finance your property depends on which advantages and disadvantages are most important to you.

12

Think Like a Lender to Get the Financing You Want

In the end, it's not equities, bonds, commodities or real estate which will help you achieve financial freedom. It's your knowledge of money which will make you rich and help you always stay wealthy and financially free.
–www.geckoandfly.com

As a commercial mortgage broker, I find it fascinating to go through the process of identifying worthy loan opportunities. It's not always obvious which are the winners and the losers. A commercial mortgage broker or loan officer can waste a lot of time if he or she doesn't choose wisely which deals to work on. After all, we don't get paid unless the loan closes. So it's critical to our financial well-being to focus on those loan opportunities that have the highest probability of closing. I have seen my peers waste several weeks, if not months, on loan requests that I intuitively knew up-front had little or no chance of closing. It's painful to watch this happen to your peers, and it's even worse to experience firsthand.

THE STEPS IN SEPARATING THE WINNERS FROM THE LOSERS

Over years of experience, successful mortgage professionals acquire a sixth sense about which real estate loan requests can ultimately be financed. The process of finding properties that have a high probability of getting financed goes something like this:

- ➤ It usually begins with a telephone call, many times from a person I've never met, who has been referred to me.
- ➤ I try my best to patiently listen to their request. I ask probing questions to draw out the issues that will make or break this deal. Usually the deal ends with this first conversation as typically I identify a significant flaw in the deal. I try my best to tell them as gently as possible that I'm not the right commercial mortgage broker for their loan request. If possible, I then refer them to someone I think can help them.
- ➤ But sometimes, usually in about one in six conversations, I end the conversation requesting their documentation so I can get a better look at the deal.
- ➤ Once I get their documentation, I underwrite the property and the borrower. I use the metrics that the typical lender will use to evaluate the loan opportunity.
- ➤ I then visit the property to see firsthand its condition and its neighborhood.

Once I've completed this process, my deal radar kicks into overdrive. I try my best to discover what makes this deal a truly good opportunity so that lenders will have no choice but to say yes.

Finding "The Hook"

As a rule, lenders are very conservative when it comes to risk-taking. They have what I like to refer to as a "belt and suspenders" approach to lending. To avoid risk, they look at the loan through redundant safety procedures, like a man who wears both a belt and suspenders to ensure his pants stay up.

Another word for "safety procedures" is what I call finding "the hook." I politely ignore the sales pitch that the prospective borrower makes about why this is such a good loan opportunity. Instead, I go fishing for the hook that I believe will snare the lender's interest. Here are several examples of finding the hook. The borrower:

➢ Agrees to sign personal recourse. He has a strong personal financial statement with substantial liquidity in proportion to the financing request.

➢ Is willing to put in all or a majority of the cash/equity required in the deal instead of a group of passive investors with minimal real estate experience.

➢ Has an excellent track record owning and managing that particular property type with decades of experience.

➢ Is requesting a very low leveraged loan.

These are just a few hooks and the more obvious ones. A good mortgage professional has the uncanny ability of finding the less obvious hooks that can change the outcome of a loan request from no to yes. Such professionals are the unsung heroes of our business. Many times the borrowers don't even realize what a service these professionals have provided them.

Commercial Mortgage Professionals Are Hook Finders

It's fairly typical for a client to request a loan with all the bells and whistles that they heard one of their peers just received. Many times they say it with something of an attitude, such as "If you don't get me these incredibly good loan terms, I'll go to your competition who'll get them for me." What they don't realize is, for their friend to have received such a smokin' deal, the lender was able to identify the hook that made those rates and terms possible. It's not enough to say that the real estate market is hot or that a specific property type is a "can't miss." We need a hook! And that is what commercial mortgage brokers do for a living. We are professional hook finders.

QUESTIONS TO ANSWER BEFORE CHOOSING
THE RIGHT PREPAYMENT PENALTY

A discussion on getting the best possible loan for your property would be incomplete without talking about prepayment penalties. There are prepayment penalty traps that you, the borrower, need to be aware of so you can avoid choosing a loan that you will later regret.

On a regular basis, I am contacted by property owners who want to refinance their properties. When I ask them if their existing loan has a prepayment penalty, many times they can't recall. I tell them the first thing they need to do is review their loan documents to find out what their current prepayment penalty is. When they call me back and tell me the type of prepay, I frequently have to be the bearer of bad news. As much as I would like to refinance their property, the size of prepayment penalty precludes that from happening. But I'm jumping the gun. Let's begin with the basics about prepayment penalties, and then you'll understand why many times I have to give the borrower this bad news.

There are two rules of thumb about prepayment penalties:

1.   The longer the fixed interest rate, the longer the prepayment penalty.

This is just plain common sense. If you request a five-year fixed rate, your prepayment penalty will be five years or less. If you request a ten-year fixed rate, your prepayment penalty will be for ten years or less. I'm surprised at how many borrowers regularly ask for the best of both worlds. They want the longest fixed rate interest rate possible, *and* they want no prepayment penalty, but they will grudgingly accept a short prepayment penalty. You can have one or the other. You can't have both.

2.   Lenders that have the most competitive interest rates generally have the worst prepayment penalties.

Here are the three most common types of prepayment penalties:

1.   **Step-Down.** This type of prepayment penalty is a gradually declining penalty over the term of the loan. It is the most common type of prepayment penalty, and it has the advantage of being easy to calculate.

A typical ten-year term might have the following prepayment penalty: 5-5-4-3-2-1-1-0-0-0. In this example, in the first two years of the loan, the borrower's penalty will be five percent of the existing loan balance. And if the borrower can wait to pay the loan off during the seventh year or later, the borrower will avoid paying a prepayment penalty altogether.

2. **Yield Maintenance.** This type of prepayment penalty protects the lender against a decline in interest rates. In an environment where interest rates are declining, borrowers typically try to refinance their loans to reduce the interest rate on their debt.

   ➤ If the loan is paid off early at a lower interest rate than when the original loan was closed, the lender loses a high-yielding investment and gets, in return, a lower rate of return on it. To reduce the effect of an early payoff, lenders often require that the borrower provide compensation, called yield maintenance.

   ➤ The yield maintenance prepayment penalty calculates the net present value of the remaining interest due on the loan to the end of the prepayment period. The loan payoff discount rate would be the difference between the new interest rate and the original mortgage's interest rate. The difference between the two cash flows for the remaining of the balance of the original loan term, discounted to the present, is the yield maintenance prepayment penalty.

3. **Defeasance**. Defeasance is the substitution of the current collateral (the property) with US Treasuries that exactly mimic the stream of payments promised at the origination of the loan. The borrower's property is released in exchange for this new collateral.

   ➤ If Treasury rates rise above the original mortgage rate, the borrower benefits from this, because the price of Treasuries will fall, and the borrower will be able to setup a portfolio that mimics the original cash flows at a lower price than the amount that would have had to be repaid.

   ➤ With yield maintenance, the note is paid off. But with defeasance, the note continues to term. Defeasance does not change anything about the cash inflows to the lender. While yield maintenance penalizes the lender when Treasury rates fall, fluctuations in the Treasury rates do not affect the lender using defeasance.

Also, there are some lenders that have lockout periods at the beginning of the loan that will not allow you to pay off the loan. Generally, a lockout period is for one or two years. After the lockout period expires, the borrower can prepay the loan. Lenders with a lockout period generally have yield maintenance for a prepayment penalty.

Some lenders will allow you to pay down up to 20 percent of the loan balance in any given year without incurring a prepayment penalty. If your goal is to pay off the loan as soon as possible, this is a perfect prepayment option to have.

Now that you know the basics on prepayment penalties, you're ready to make two important decisions about financing. The first question you have to ask yourself is, *How long do I plan to own this property?* If you really don't know, then go with a shorter fixed rate loan. You'll get the advantage of a lower interest rate and a prepayment penalty that will be less onerous if you plan to sell or refinance sooner than you thought you would.

The second question you have to ask yourself is, *Do I really want to choose the loan quote with the lowest interest rate if it comes with an awful prepayment penalty?* Many times the answer to this question is a resounding no. As you can sense, not all prepayment penalties are equally bad. Many times that smokin' interest rate comes with either a yield maintenance or defeasance prepayment penalty.

The good news is that you don't need to understand the definitions of yield maintenance and defeasance to make an informed decision (you can breathe a sigh of relief now). All you need to understand is this very important point: *You will never, ever pay off a loan with yield maintenance or defeasance.* Why? Because the cost of the prepayment penalty is so egregious that no sane person would do it. Even in the last year of the prepayment penalty, when the cost of prepaying the loan will be at its lowest, the cost is still prohibitive. You may be wondering how expensive could it really be? Unfortunately, you don't have the ability to calculate a yield maintenance or defeasance prepayment penalty. It's that complicated. Contact your existing lender to request an estimate of what it will cost to pay off your loan early. But when they call you back with the answer, be sure you're sitting down. The cost is so absurdly high that you won't even be angry with the answer. Instead, you'll be astounded, and you'll start chuckling to yourself.

My advice regarding prepayment penalties is simple. Regardless of the type of prepayment penalty, make sure that it in no way impedes on your time horizon for refinancing or selling your property. And under no circumstances should you get a loan that has yield maintenance or defeasance if you think there is even the remotest possibility that you will want to sell or refinance your property before the loan comes due since the cost of the prepayment penalty will be so expensive. Don't handcuff yourself with a prepayment penalty that has the potential of preventing you from making sound financing or investment decisions in the future for the sake of a slightly better interest rate or a longer fixed rate period. It's not worth it.

TO MAKE YOUR PROPERTY LENDER-FRIENDLY, AVOID THESE SIX THINGS

I'm surprised how often I am asked to find financing for a property that, for one reason or another, is obviously not financeable. It's as if the borrower wants the lender to forgo the use of common sense. I'm going to let you in on a little secret: IT ISN'T GOING TO HAPPEN! Anyone who is at all knowledgeable about real estate lending realizes that lenders are risk averse. They are not in business to take on more risk than is absolutely necessary.

So if you want to either refinance your property or sell it, there are things you must do a year or two *before* financing is needed to get the property to the point where I call it "lender-friendly." Not doing so will likely make it much more difficult, if not impossible, to get a lender interested. Here are six common situations you should strive to fix:

1. **The property is in poor physical condition.** It's a big turn-off to lenders to see a property poorly maintained. Why would a lender refinance a property for a borrower who is unwilling to maintain his property? If you want to refinance a property that has a lot of deferred maintenance, you better have an excellent explanation as to why it's in

poor condition. Better yet, you should get the big-ticket items fixed prior to refinancing your property.

2. **The occupancy rate for the property is below market**, calling into question the seller's property management company's ability to professionally manage the property. And if the property is self-managed, you're in deep trouble. If the property is for sale, some sellers or listing brokers think that providing a rent guarantee on the unoccupied space will satisfy a lender's concern. Wrong! It does just the opposite. It's a great big red flag that something is wrong with the property. A better solution is to offer as much free rent as needed to get the vacant space occupied. Offer the free rent at the beginning of the lease. Once the free rent has burned off, then refinance or put the property up for sale. You still need to disclose the free rent to the lender, but it is much better to have your property at stabilized occupancy with free rent than to have a property with a high vacancy rate.

3. **Operating expenses are well above normal** for a property of that age and condition. You need to investigate if there is a reason for this. Is it an anomaly? Are some ongoing maintenance expenses actually capital expenditures? If so, can you explain why? If you can determine that the additional expenses are costly one-time expenses, then identify those expenses and remove them from your operating expenses, explaining in detail why you removed them. If you rush to refinance the property with higher than normal operating expenses, it will likely lower the loan amount because of the lender's minimum debt coverage requirement. And if you're trying to sell the property, the value of the property will be adversely impacted because the NOI for the property will be lower than it should be. Worst-case scenario, the lower NOI could reduce the buyer's loan amount and thereby increase the equity required by the buyer beyond what he is willing to invest in the property, which will kill your sale.

4. **Most tenants are on a month-to-month basis** (not as much of a concern for apartment renters) or have only one or two years remaining on the term of their lease. Most lenders will not accept rollover risk. Again,

proposing a rent guarantee on those tenants whose leases have expired or will expire shortly is a big turn-off to lenders. One way to mitigate risk is to identify when each tenant originally moved in. If they have been tenants at the property for ten or more years, then it is much less likely they will plan to move once the lease expires. But the best thing to do before you sell or refinance your property is to get as many tenants released for as long as possible. Once you've minimized the rollover risk, then seek financing.

5. **Too much existing debt on the property, making it too highly leveraged.** I occasionally see properties that currently don't support the debt that was put on the property prior to the Great Recession. The good news is that the owner has been faithfully paying his monthly mortgage payments. The bad news is that, in order to refinance his property, the owner will have to pay down the existing mortgage—that is, pay cash at closing to pay off the existing loan. Unfortunately, many owners are unable or unwilling to do that.

6. **Not keeping good records on the property.** A property owner should keep separate books on each property he owns. Unfortunately, I sometimes see comingled funds with other properties or with the owner's personal accounts. Bookkeeping needs to be clear and accurate so a lender can assess the property's performance since the lender needs to know if the property can support the proposed mortgage payment. The chances of getting financing are slim without accurate historical operating statements, a current rent roll, and a list of capital improvements over the past few years.

Remember, you're trying to get the lender as comfortable as possible with financing the property. You're asking the lender to lend you or your buyer lots of money. Make sure to take some common sense steps prior to requesting a loan that makes it easy for the lender to say yes.

TEN UNDERWRITING GUIDELINES
LENDERS USE TO QUALIFY BORROWERS

Borrower underwriting guidelines have changed dramatically in recent years. In the good old days, prior to the Great Recession, lenders did a very cursory job of underwriting the borrower. They focused almost exclusively on the pros and cons of the property. And if they liked the risks associated with the property, it was very likely the loan would be approved with only a cursory look at the borrower.

In recent years, all this has changed. Lenders have upped their borrower documentation considerably, requiring an extensive amount of information on the borrower.

But some borrowers are still thinking they are in pre-Great Recession times with the lenders. You must understand that those days are long past. Under today's lender guidelines, the borrower needs to be proactive about providing their personal documentation at the same time as the property documentation. Doing so strongly suggests that you, the borrower, are a professional, savvy investor. Instead of slowly dripping the required documents over a couple of weeks or so, have them all prepared so you can give them to lenders all at once.

Here are ten borrower underwriting guidelines that lenders use to qualify you. You need to know each one and be ready to address them:

1. **Minimum Net Worth to Loan Ratio** – Provide the lender with a complete, professional-looking personal financial statement. Each lender has different requirements, but lenders typically require the borrower's net worth to be equal to or greater than the loan amount. Some require a borrower's net worth to be as much as two times the proposed loan amount. Before you send your financial statement, ask the lender what the minimum net worth to loan ratio is. If your net worth exceeds this ratio, then proceed with sending him all your personal documentation.

2. **Global Cash Flow** – Many lenders are now creating a global cash flow from the borrower's real-estate-owned (REO) schedule. Lenders want to see if the prospective borrower's combined real estate portfolio is generating a positive cash flow or slowly draining him of all his cash. An REO schedule shows all the details that cover the following:

➢ gross potential income

➢ other income

➢ vacancy and bad debt loss

➢ operating expenses

➢ net operating income

➢ debt service

➢ net cash flow after debt service

Total the combined net operating income (NOI) of all the borrower's properties and divide by the annual debt service of all his or her properties. Ideally, a lender would like to see a combined debt coverage ratio (DCR) well in excess of 1.25 to 1.

For example, let's say the combined NOI of the borrower's real estate equals $500,000 and his combined annual debt service equals $400,000. Therefore, the borrower has a DCR of 1.25 to 1. Some lenders will also look at each individual property on the borrower's REO schedule, and if there are one or more properties that have a negative cash flow—that is, the annual debt service exceeds the property's NOI—then the borrower will have to explain why this is so and what steps are being taken to correct the situation.

Prepare the REO schedule before you begin talking to lenders so when they ask for it, it's ready for them. If you need a copy of a REO schedule, contact me and I'll email you one.

3. **Personal Cash Flow** – This analysis focuses on the sponsor's personal income and expenses. It is calculated by totaling annual income from wages, interest income, real estate investments, and so on, and then dividing the total into all living expenses and personal debt, including mortgage payments, auto loans, credit card debt, and the like. This ratio should be better than 1 to 1.

4. **Cash to Revolving Debt Ratio** – The underwriter also looks closely at the amount of revolving debt and compares it to the amount of cash (not including retirement accounts) shown on the borrower's balance sheet. The amount of cash should exceed the amount of revolving debt, and the more it does the better the borrower's rating.

5. **Global Liquidity** – Divide the total cash shown on the borrower's balance sheet by the proposed monthly debt service for the new loan. This will tell you the number of months of liquidity the borrower has available should something go terribly wrong, resulting in the property being unable to pay the mortgage payment from the cash flow off the property. Most lenders would like to see, at a very minimum, six to nine months of a liquidity cushion. So if the monthly mortgage payment is $10,000, the borrower better have $60,000 to $90,000 in cash reserves in order to qualify for the loan.

6. **Global Leverage** – The total real estate debt divided by the total estimated value of the borrower's real estate portfolio should not exceed 75 percent. The less leveraged the borrower's real estate is, the better his or her rating.

7. **Credit Rating and Explanations of Thirty-Day Late Payments** – Run a credit report on yourself before you start looking for a lender. Find out your credit score. Most lenders require that your credit score be a minimum of 680. If yours is not that high, you better have a good explanation. You also need to explain every payment that is thirty days late or more. Put it in writing before you're asked.

8. **Explain Past Tax Liens, Judgments, and Litigation** – Have written explanations with backup documentation already prepared before you sign the application. Give the prospective lender your explanations and have him verify in advance of signing your application that your explanations are satisfactory and will not impact loan approval. Do this before you sign the application when you have the most negotiating power, not after when you have little or none.

9. **Tax Returns, Not Just Schedule 1040s, Signed and Dated, Including All K-1s** – Lenders want all of your federal tax returns, not parts of them. This includes providing all of your K-1s. To speed up the process, get this done correctly the first time.

10. **Real Estate Experience** – Ideally, an applicant should have several years of experience owning or managing commercial real estate. The more

years the better. Without experience, a property management company will likely be required.

One of the truest statements ever uttered about real estate is "Time kills deals." A lengthy, drawn out, loan-underwriting process will at the very least move your deal to the bottom of the pile. It has the potential of killing the deal altogether. Many of these ten borrower underwriting guidelines can be verified quickly if the borrower anticipates what the lender is going to require and provides it in a professionally looking package.

THREE OTHER ISSUES THAT CAN TORPEDO YOUR FINANCING CHANCES

Before we move on, there are three other issues that can torpedo a borrower's chance of getting financing that has nothing to do with the lender's underwriting criteria for qualifying the borrower. It has a lot to do with the borrower's attitude.

1. Unrealistic Expectations of the Borrower

It's surprising to me how often I hear borrowers requesting loan terms that are not being offered in the market, including:

➢ higher than normal loan-to-value expectation;
➢ a longer fixed rate loan term than lenders offer;
➢ unrealistically low expectations for the costs associated with financing the property; and
➢ an expectation of little or no prepayment penalty for fixed rate loans.

2. Violating the Golden Rule of Lending

I've come across some real estate property owners who act as if they are God's gift to real estate. You know who I'm talking about. They don't think that the rules of financing apply to them because they're special. Right. Of course, they're not so privileged.

Recall the Golden Rule of Lending: "He who has the gold makes the rules." If you want a loan, you must comply with what the lender is asking for in the way of documentation. Some say that what the lender requires is intrusive and unnecessary. I will admit at times this can be true. But the question still remains: Do you want the loan or not? If so, don't argue with the lender's requirements. It will get you nowhere.

3. Going to the Wrong Lender

I will often ask a borrower what lenders he has already talked to about getting a loan. Once I hear the lenders he's contacted, I find it obvious why he is still searching for financing: the borrower doesn't know the right lenders to contact in order to get the best rate and terms for his property.

These three issues will inevitably doom the borrower's chances to finance his property. If instead the borrower placed his trust in a qualified commercial mortgage broker, the broker could guide him through the loan process to a successful conclusion. The goal of the borrower and the commercial mortgage broker should be to make the lender's underwriting process flow as smoothly as possible to avoid ever hearing the words, "I'm sorry to inform you that your loan has been turned down."

THE TIME OF YEAR IS MORE IMPORTANT THAN YOU THINK

They say that timing is everything. Well, this certainly holds true when it comes to financing commercial real estate. There are times during the year when trying to get a loan financed is pure misery, and there are times when the financing gods are looking down benevolently on you. There is an optimal time to get things financed. Shown below are the worst times and then the best times to get your property financed.

Worst Times to Finance Real Estate

JUNE 10TH THROUGH LABOR DAY

If you haven't signed your loan application before summer starts, good luck! Summer is the time when kids are out of school and families take long vacations. Loan officers, underwriters, loan processors, real estate brokers, commercial mortgage brokers, attorneys, appraisers, and the like all lose focus during the summer months. As a result, the financing process slows to a crawl, or so it seems.

NOVEMBER 1ST THROUGH YEAR-END

If your loan is not expected to close before year-end, your deal will go to the bottom of the pile. All the focus during the end of the year is to work on deals that will close so loan officers can make their quotas and, for those who have had a good year, to make their bonuses.

Best Times to Finance Real Estate

FIRST QUARTER

The best time of the year to start the financing process is during the first quarter. Bankers are refreshed after the holidays and eager to start working on their annual quotas in order to achieve their year-end bonuses. Most insurance companies will be back in the market ready to lend. As the year progresses, they become more and more selective on property type and quality of transaction.

LABOR DAY THROUGH OCTOBER 31ST

People are back from vacations, kids are in school, and lenders are again eager to get their last round of deals started for the year so that they close before the holiday season.

NOVEMBER 1ST THROUGH THE 15TH

To paraphrase Charles Dickens, the first two weeks of November *are the best of times and the worst of times.* No sane loan officer should commit to closing a loan in less than sixty days. But those loan officers who haven't reached their quota or have but want to increase their bonuses even more, go into warp speed, trying to cram in the final deals for the year. If the moon and the stars line up perfectly or the loan officers are just plain lucky, they succeed at securing the financing.

I once had a client who had to close his real estate purchase before the end of the year or he would experience adverse tax consequences. There were less than fifty days to the end of the year, and the deal was not yet under application. I hadn't closed a loan that year under seventy days, and most had taken considerably longer. Still, four lenders committed to closing this deal before year-end. The client chose a lender, and it happened as promised. This tells me there are a lot of hungry loan officers who want to get deals closed no matter what it takes.

So when is the best time to finance real estate? Whenever your loan officer is highly motivated to get the deal done.

THE TRUTH ABOUT RISING INTEREST RATES

In the back of the minds of most commercial real estate investors is the never-ending question, *When will interest rates go back up?* We have collectively fretted over rising interest rates for almost four decades. And yet the truth is, those who have locked in long-term interest rates over the years have been the big losers. Interest rates have continued declining while the fixed rate stays at the higher interest rate. It would have been in the borrowers' best interests if they had chosen a short-term variable rate or even a five-year fixed rate than to have locked in a ten-year fixed rate loan or longer. Thinking rates certainly have to go back up, those who locked in the longer fixed term rates over the years have been found to be consistently wrong. I know of no exceptions.

So why do so many people fixate on finding a fixed rate? I think part of the reason is human nature. We are always fighting the last battle, and for most of us over fifty years of age, the last great battle was inflation. We remember when our money market account was giving us 18 percent interest. We remember the adverse effects of runaway inflation. Likewise, for those among us who grew up during the Great Depression, their lifetime battle was hunger and poverty, so even when the US prospered after World War II, they were still overly careful about spending their money.

So where are we at this moment in time? Will rates eventually rise? Yes, they will. That's because interest rates fluctuate over time. And yet, as of this moment, I find no reason to believe interest rates will rise. It's just as likely that they will go down or possibly stay within a range that we have recently seen. Here's why.

Interest rates are not controlled by the Federal Reserve, the federal government, or some nefarious secret society. Yes, the Federal Reserve does set the overnight interest rate between banks, but increasing this rate has little or no impact on five-year, ten-year, or thirty-year US treasury yields. So when you hear about the Federal Reserve chairperson proposing to increase the federal funds rate at the next meeting of the Federal Open Market Committee, it really doesn't make any difference.

That said, the Fed does have the ability to manipulate interest rates. They did this in spades with quantitative easing. To get us out of the Great Recession, the Fed purchased massive quantities of government bonds and other financial assets. The result was a lowering of US Treasury yields. But even then the Fed still had to work within the bounds of the law of supply and demand. Here's how it works. It all begins with the US Treasury needing to sell bonds because the federal government is spending more money than it is taking in in tax revenues. Hence, the growing national debt.

At some point, we will have to pay the piper for spending more than we take in. Who knows when that will happen? Likely you and I will be long dead and gone when that happens. So I fear for my grandchildren, but I digress.

I don't pretend to understand the government bond auction process. Suffice it to say that the US Treasury Department auctions off government bonds at different maturity dates from one month to thirty years. For example, let's say the US Treasury auctions off $100 billion of ten-year treasury notes. One of three things will happen:

1. If demand for the ten-year bond equals the supply, the asking interest rate (whatever that treasury yield is at the moment) remains the same.
2. If demand for the ten-year bond exceeds supply, then the asking interest rate trends lower until the demand at the lower treasury yield levels off to meet the supply.
3. If demand for the ten-year bond is less than the supply, then the asking interest rate will trend higher until demand improves so supply and demand are equalized.

That's how it works.

So let's get back to the quantitative easing program that the Fed employed to stimulate the economy out of the Great Recession. When the Fed purchased huge quantities of US treasury bonds, they artificially increased the demand for treasuries, thereby lowering treasury yields.

When Donald Trump won the US presidency, the ten-year treasury rate zoomed up seventy basis points over night. The reason given at the time for the increase was that the economic policies of a Trump administration would be good for the US economy. That seems to disprove my thinking that treasury rates are all about supply and demand. If true, it would poke a big hole in my theory. But this explanation is incorrect. What really happened was that China was going through a severe liquidity crisis at the time, which required the People's Bank of China to sell a massive amount of US treasury bonds. So what happens when the supply of US bonds increases? The interest rate must increase to increase the demand commensurately. And that is exactly what happened when China dumped US treasuries. Our treasury rates zoomed up overnight.

There is one more thing to consider in order to understand where interest rates are going in the years ahead. The Federal Reserve is only one of several central banks worldwide. In order to stimulate the Japanese and European economies over the past several years, the central banks of Japan and Europe have artificially lowered interest rates to near zero using their version of quantitative easing. So let's say you're a Japanese citizen and you have a choice of investing your excess cash in a Japanese ten-year bond at 0.2 percent or investing your cash in a US Treasury bond at 2.0 percent. Which would you choose? Now let's also say that the US dollar is appreciating 10 percent in value when compared to the Japanese yen. So instead of a Japanese citizen getting 2 percent return on his US treasury note, he now receives a 12 percent return. If you were that person, which option would you choose? It's a no-brainer, isn't it? And that's just one example of what's been happening.

So to understand future treasury rates, you need to understand the concept of the law of supply and demand. As long as US Treasury yields are higher than bond yields from other nations, US treasury rates will continue to stay low because demand for our treasuries will remain high. It's as simple as that. Until the global situation changes, US Treasury yields will likely remain low.

So the next time a lender or mortgage broker encourages you to lock in that low rate for ten years or longer, think twice. Is that really a good decision? History proves otherwise.

Part 3

Managing Commercial Real Estate

13

On-Site Management Decisions That Help You Avoid Costly Mistakes

Some people don't believe in heroes,
but they haven't met a property manager.
–Anonymous

The next important step in the process is deciding who will manage your property. You have three options:

➤ Self-manage your property
➤ Hire an onsite manager who reports directly to you, or
➤ Hire a property management company to manage the property for you

There is no right option here. Which you choose all depends on how much time and effort you want to spend on your property.

For those property owners who self-manage their properties, I say more power to you.

From my perspective, I've always believed that the best tool in my toolbox is my checkbook. I've learned the hard way over the years that I should avoid doing things that others can do better, faster, and sometimes cheaper. For me, property management falls into that category. I leave it up to the professionals so I can focus my time on things for which I'm better suited.

What to Consider When Choosing a Property Management Company

In the course of my work as a commercial mortgage broker, I inspect lots of properties, talk with numerous on-site managers, and get to review many different types of operating statements. Over the years, I've gotten to know the good property management companies from those that are grossly incompetent.

What makes a good property management firm? To find out, there are numerous questions you could ask. However, I would focus my questioning on three broad categories.

How Do They Charge for Their Services?

I'm aware of at least three different ways that property management firms charge their clients:

1. The most common way is a property management fee based on effective gross income. Is their management fee competitive with what is being offered in the market?

2. Sometimes property management companies will charge you a hidden fee when using their maintenance personnel. This can happen when a property doesn't have a full-time maintenance man, and the management company's maintenance man is contracted out at an hourly rate whenever needed. Does the management company charge the owner of the property an hourly rate equal to their cost of employing their maintenance man, or do they charge the property owner at an hourly rate that's well above what it actually costs the property management company to have this person employed by them? Many times the property management company is charging the property owner an hourly rate that is well above what it's costing them to have this employee on staff. If so, they are making money on you every time a maintenance item is getting fixed on your property. Just by looking at the maintenance and repair costs, I can usually tell which property management companies are charging an excessive hourly rate for their maintenance personnel.

3. Do they charge the owner of a property an asset management fee? If so, is the fee a reasonable expense for the services rendered, or is it really a hidden profit center for the property management company?

Are Their Operating Statements Easily Readable and Disclose All Important Information?

The quality of operating statements I see varies widely from handwritten to very detailed computer-generated reports. Here are some questions about the income and expense items that concern matters I like to watch:

➤ Do the operating statements begin with gross potential rent or with effective gross income? In other words, do the statements show vacancy, bad debt, and concessions? If the statements do not show gross potential rent, then owners can't readily determine how much vacancy the property is experiencing.

➤ Do the operating statements show all payroll expenses, including free rent?

An owner cannot make informed decisions on his property without having accurate and detailed operating statements that show the good, the bad, and the ugly.

An owner once told me that his property didn't have a vacancy problem. He was shocked when I informed him that his property for the past year averaged 12 percent vacancy in a market whose average vacancy rate was less than 5 percent. He didn't know he had a vacancy issue and bad debt problem because it wasn't explicitly shown on the property's operating statement, only the rent received. Those primitive operating statements were hiding the cost of vacancy and bad debt.

Can I Help Select My On-Site Manager?

No matter how good the property management company is, the on-site manager has the most influence on a property's performance. And the only way to determine the quality of on-site managers is to observe how well they do their job. I would focus on these issues:

➢ How is the property's curb appeal? Is trash found lying on the grounds picked up regularly? Are trash enclosures hidden and well maintained so as not to be an eyesore? Are flowerbeds weed-free and attractive?

➢ How well do the on-site managers stay on top of collecting monthly rents? Some managers are passive about collecting rents, which, over time, will cause collection problems. Other managers promptly post notices and have a sharp eye out for renters who pay slowly.

➢ How quickly do the on-site managers get a unit ready to be re-rented? In a tight rental market, every day a unit is waiting to be cleaned is money out of your pocket. Ask the manager what type of system she has for getting units market ready.

A good on-site manager is worth her weight in gold and can have a significant impact on the property's cash flow. In many instances, your choice of a property management company and an on-site property manager can make the difference between a property that does well and one that limps along.

REASONS FOR FIRING YOUR ON-SITE PROPERTY MANAGER

For large multi-tenanted properties to be well managed, it requires three levels of oversight. As the saying goes, "A chain is only as strong as its weakest link" is definitely true for property management. If any one of these three levels of oversight is done poorly, the property's performance will suffer.

The three levels of property oversight are: (1) the on-site manager; (2) the off-site property management company; and (3) the owner. Smaller properties with less tenants do not need an on-site manager. But apartments with twenty or more units may need on-sight management, as well as large retail, office, and sometimes industrial properties. On-site managers will maximize a property's performance.

On-site managers are generally overworked and underpaid. Often they don't get the credit they deserve for a well maintained property. If you have an on-site property manager who is performing her job well, pay her accordingly. My management philosophy is to pay on-site managers 20 percent more than the going rate for their position. You never want to have a good on-site manger quit because he or she can make a few more dollars working elsewhere. Not paying them well is truly penny-wise and pound-foolish.

Of course, not all on-site managers perform well. So when is it appropriate to fire the on-site manager? There are six reasons for firing your on-site property manager.

1. **Consistently not maintaining the property's appearance**

   A property's appearance is the first impression a prospective renter has of your rental property. Is it inviting, or does it leave a poor impression? The property needs to look clean and neat. A good on-site manager when walking the property should be in the habit of always picking up trash that is lying around.

2. **Not following the rental policies to the letter**

   Rent is due on the first but late by the fifth day of the month. No exceptions. Renters who don't pay on time are always assessed a late fee regardless of their reason. If you don't consistently charge a late fee, you remove the incentive for their paying the rent on time.

3. **Not keeping out-of-control tenants on a short leash**

   Every property I've ever owned or managed has had at least one problem tenant. These tenants act as if the rules don't apply to them. The on-site manager needs to let these problem tenants know that they must abide by the rules. If you let problem tenants run roughshod over the property, the good tenants will eventually move out.

4. **Ignoring maintenance repair requests**

   A colleague of mine once had an on-site manager he reluctantly fired only to discover she had a drawer full of maintenance requests that she let slide. Do you want happy tenants? Make sure maintenance repair requests are completed in a timely fashion.

5. **Beginning to consider their tenants as their friends instead of their customers**

   You can imagine how this change in thinking can result in all sorts of bad things happening at the property. One time I was refinancing a property where there was a disconnect between the property's occupancy rate, which was good, and the rent collections, which were bad, really bad. In my mind, the only way that could possibly happen is if the on-site manager was evicting several tenants for non-payment of rent, but this was not the case. After interviewing the manager, she admitted that several of the tenants were having financial difficulties and hadn't paid rent for the past few months. They had promised her that they would pay their back rent when their financial situation got better. Because the manager considered these tenants her friends, she wasn't willing to enforce the property's rental policies.

6. **Suffering from burnout, causing them to stop caring for the property**
This is the saddest reason for firing an on-site property manager. You never want this to happen. It's incumbent on the off-site property manager or the owner to recognize the beginning stages of burnout so either person can do whatever is necessary for this not to happen.

SEVEN HIDDEN COSTS MANAGING YOUR APARTMENTS

There are several categories of operating expenses necessary to maintain and manage apartments. We all know these expenses: property taxes, insurance, utility charges, maintenance and turnover costs, on-site and off-site management costs, and the like. But less well known are potential hidden costs of maintaining and managing an apartment that in large part can determine the profitability of your investment. Here they are and in no particular order.

1. The Time It Takes to Get a Unit Market-Ready

In a tight rental market, every day it takes to get a unit ready for occupancy takes money out of the owner's pocket. For example, let's say a vacant unit has a monthly rent of $1,000. If it takes two weeks to turn the unit, it's costing the owner $467 in lost rent ($1,000 ÷ 30 days x 14 days). If it takes only a week to make the unit market-ready, the shorter time to turn the unit saves the owner $234 compared to a two-week turn. I have seen vacant units stay dirty and unrentable for several weeks because the onsite staff have been focused on other issues that are not nearly as important to the property's bottom-line.

2. Mediocre or Worse On-Site Manager

The older I get, the more I realize that common sense is not common. I shudder to think of the impact of an on-site manager who lacks common sense. Sometimes a vacant unit will remain vacant for weeks because the manager is waiting for her favorite vendor to do one small part of the turn instead of hiring one of the vendor's competitors. I've seen where the on-site manager is slow to return a prospect's call about a vacant unit, resulting in the prospect going elsewhere. Sometimes a manager limits the time when a prospect can view a vacant unit so that it's convenient for the manager, not the prospect, which results in the prospect giving up on renting the unit. There are many ways an on-site manager can do significant damage to the property's profitability. I've mentioned just a few.

3. Owners Tight with Employee Compensation

Sometimes the problem is not with the on-site manager but with the owner not compensating the on-site manager well. A good employee is worth his or her weight in gold. The old adage "You get what you pay for" is very true when it comes to hiring people. Treat them with respect and pay them well so they begin to think like an owner. Incentivize them to focus on those things that you want performed well. For example, maybe you pay them an incentive for turning the unit faster than they normally do. Undercompensating your on-site manager is shortsighted, and it can cost you a lot of money.

4. Not Finding Water Leaks

Water leaks can be notoriously difficult to find. Sometimes you're not even sure you have a water leak, but the monthly bill just seems way too high. If the property has more than one building, the easiest way to determine if you have a water leak is to compare water bills between buildings. If they have the same number of units, the water bill should be more or less similar. But if one is significantly higher each month, it's likely there is a water leak in that building. Spend the money to find the leak, and be persistent until it's found.

I once had a client who was purchasing a property with a very high water bill. The first month he owned the property he discovered the source of the water leak and fixed it. Fixing the leak reduced the property's annual water bill by $30,000! He bought the property at a 6.5 percent cap rate so fixing the water leak immediately increased the value of his property by $462,000 ($30,000 ÷ 0.065). Or another way to look at it, since the seller had not found the water leak, it cost him big time.

5. Deferring Maintenance for Short-Term Profits

Do you remember the old FRAM oil filter ads on TV? The auto mechanic says to the car owner, "You can pay me now [meaning you can buy a good quality oil filter] or you can pay me later [meaning you can buy a cheap oil filter now and a new engine later]." It was a very effective ad campaign.

Some property owners haven't learned the "pay me now or pay me later" lesson. Not only will the maintenance problem not go away, but it will also get more costly to fix the longer you wait. And when you defer obvious maintenance problems, it makes a statement to the residents. It says to them you would rather have your monthly owner's distributions than maintain the property. It also makes it harder to rent to well-qualified tenants because the property looks tired, if not run-down. There are high hidden costs to pay for not maintaining your property.

6. On-Site Managers Picking Bad Residents

I'm not suggesting a manager should discriminate based on race, color, sexual orientation, and the like. I'm not even hinting at that. What I am strongly suggesting is that there is more to tenant selection than running background checks, calling previous landlords, and the like. An in-person interview can many times give you insights into a person that can't be objectively measured by the traditional tenant selection process. An on-site manager should trust his or her gut instinct. Use common sense to weed out potential problem residents before they move in. The hidden costs of problem tenants in time, money, and aggravation can be huge.

7. A Property Management Company That Nickel and Dimes You

There are property management companies in Portland, Oregon that I sense are ripping off their clients. Comparing their operating expenses on a cost per unit basis with their competitors, they are consistently $500 per unit higher for comparable properties. How do they do it? There are multiple ways. As I shared before, one of the most egregious ways is by making their maintenance staff profit centers. Instead of charging the property owner what it's costing them for the maintenance staff's wages, payroll taxes, and employee benefits, they charge significantly more—in fact, way more. So every time an owner uses their maintenance guy, they are making a profit. As owners we need to make sure the property management company we hire has a reputation for honest billing of their services.

Tackle these hidden costs head on. The overall success of your apartment as an investment depends on it.

Off-Site Management Decisions to Optimize Your Property's Performance

Real estate cannot be lost or stolen, nor can it be carried away. Purchased with common sense, paid for in full, and managed with reasonable care it is about the safest investment in the world.
–Franklin D. Roosevelt, 32nd president of the United States

Many times when there is a property management problem, it's because of the on-site manager. But sometimes it's not the fault of the on-site manager. Instead it's the property management company that's not doing an adequate job. So why and when should you drop your property management company?

WHEN TO FIRE YOUR PROPERTY MANAGEMENT COMPANY

Poor Recordkeeping

A property's operating statements are the first indicator of how well a property is functioning. They should give you a cursory snapshot of the property. Is it operating smoothly or is a problem possibly brewing?

I'll give you a real-life example. I was noticing over the last few years that turnover expenses at an apartment I was helping to refinance were extremely high. Now part of the problem was the owner had significantly raised rents over this time period which "encouraged" some of the tenants to move out. But that answer didn't completely satisfy me. So I reviewed the general ledger for the past four years. What I discovered was the same type of repair work was being done over and over again on the same units. For instance, one unit had been turned three times in four years, and each time the carpet was replaced. As we all know, carpets have a longer life expectancy than one year. And if the tenant abused the carpet, then he or she should be charged for it. Good recordkeeping identified a problem with management. I discovered that the company was making unnecessary carpet replacements as well as other unnecessary repairs.

Unfortunately, many times the recordkeeping is so rudimentary that there is no way to find out why expenses are out of control. This is why you select a property management company that provides detailed operating statements. Good recordkeeping can reveal whether or not your property is being well managed.

Consistently Not Keeping Expenses within Budget

An operating budget is the roadmap for how the owner wants the property to be managed and maintained. There are times when things happen that are completely outside the control of the property management company that can blowup a budget. Also, an operating budget can be unrealistic from the get-go. It can be a pretense that both the owner and the property management company go through once a year as an exercise in futility.

That said, I've observed property management companies that have made absolutely no effort in keeping operating expenses in line with the budget. The example I mentioned above about replacing the carpet in the same unit three times in four years illustrates my point. A mortgage broker shouldn't be the first person to point out an out-of-control budget. A good off-site property manager should have recognized this problem long before I did, but unfortunately that wasn't the case. Instead, she was clueless.

Not Adequately Training the On-Site Manager

As a mortgage broker, I visit many properties every year. I'm often shocked by the on-site manager's lack of professionalism. It's embarrassing to see how poorly some managers represent the owner with their poor appearance and overall demeanor. It calls into question whether they have been adequately trained by the property management company. On-site managers should know the appropriate policies and procedures about:

> ➤ proper attire for on-site staff
> ➤ leasing
> ➤ qualifying prospective tenants
> ➤ rent collection
> ➤ overseeing turnover
> ➤ completing work orders in a timely manner
> ➤ maintaining a property's appearance

And these are just a few of the essentials.

If the on-site manager does not know such things, the fault is not hers. The responsibility falls on the shoulders of the property management company for not training properly.

Lax Oversight of the On-Site Manager

The property management company needs to regularly shop the on-site manager. A shopper is someone who pretends to be a prospective renter but in reality is there to observe the professionalism of the on-site manager. How is her appearance? How well does she greet the prospective tenant? How well does she show a market-ready unit to the prospect? The shopper especially pays attention to whether the on-site manager tries to overcome any leasing objections presented to her.

The property management company also needs to regularly inspect

> ➤ the property's appearance,
> ➤ the lease files for all the paperwork being completed properly, and

   ➢ how long it takes for a unit to be made market-ready.

A good property management company does of all of this and much more.

More Concerned with Maintaining a High Occupancy Rate Than Raising Rents

If your property is consistently full, especially in a market that averages 5 percent or more vacancy, your rents are too low. Below market rents are a hidden cost. Sure it's nice not having the turnover costs of a vacant unit, but if you do the math, raising all of your rents to market usually pays for the few units that end up being vacated because of the higher rental rates.

An apartment owner was consistently told by the property management company that his property's current rents were at the top of the market. Raising rents, they said, would cause a mass move out of tenants. The property management company was replaced a short while later. The new property management company raised rents an average of $250 per unit. And more importantly, the property's occupancy did not suffer from the hefty rent increases.

Sometimes property management companies are more concerned with keeping the property occupied than maximizing revenue. Increased vacancy requires more effort than they want to expend. In their mind, it's just easier keeping the property full. They think, *How can an owner have a problem with a property that's always full?* But this perspective actually works against the interests of the owner.

Lots of Employee Turnover

I'm a part owner in a small office building. We have had four off-site property managers in the three years we've owned the property. When that happens, ongoing issues lose out as the new manager needs to relearn what the previous manager was doing to solve them. If the property management company has high employee turnover, something is wrong with how they treat their employees, how well they compensate them, or both.

I asked the last off-site manager why he was leaving. He said he had a portfolio of thirteen properties he had been managing, and he felt he could adequately manage just three. This high turnover of managers suggested to me that I needed to look for a new property management company.

Employee problems don't go away until someone addresses the issues they raise.

THE #1 MISTAKE PROPERTY OWNERS CAN MAKE

A very wise person once said, "A cord of three strands is not easily broken." This saying is definitely true when it comes to property management. As was stated previously, for large multi-tenanted properties to be well maintained, it requires three levels of oversight: the on-site manager, the off-site management company, and the property owner.

Comic strip character *Pogo* once said, "We have met the enemy and he is us." That is certainly true when it comes to owning commercial real estate. You can be your own worst enemy by how you manage your properties. Whether you self-manage, hire an on-site manager who reports to you, or hire a property management company, there is one thing you can do to optimize the performance of your properties. But before I tell you what that is, let me explain how I learned this essential tip to managing commercial real estate.

My Experience Managing Apartments

In a former life, I was both an on-site and off-site property manager for newly constructed class-A apartments located in Nashville, Tennessee and Atlanta, Georgia. I managed three class-A apartments totaling over five hundred units. I had twenty-three employees under me. My three years of property management experience was like drinking from a fire hose. I learned so much about human nature, how to manage people, how to keep a property running smoothly, and, most importantly, how to keep my tenants happy. Quite frankly, it was the longest three years of my life! My personality bent was not suited to being a property manager, so when an opportunity came to get back into the financing side of real estate, I jumped at it. That said, I have nothing but respect, bordering on awe, for those on-site property managers who do their job well.

You Get What You Inspect, Not What You Expect

The most important lesson I learned while I was a property manager was *you get what you inspect, not what you expect.* Not until I started inspecting whatever task I requested did my employees realize I meant what I said. Sure they would go through the motions and do whatever I asked, but most of the time it was not to an acceptable level. But when I started inspecting their work, all of a sudden the quality of their performance improved significantly.

The same was true with my kids during their formative years. If I asked them to clean their bedrooms, their performance was always mediocre at best until ol' dad inspected their rooms.

All of this goes to what I have found to be the number one mistake most real estate owners make—namely, *they do a very poor job overseeing their on-site managers or the property management companies with whom they contract.* A property owner can significantly improve the performance of his properties by doing a better job overseeing the property management of those properties. Passive owners are asking for trouble. It isn't by accident that out-of-state owners are more likely than in-state owners to have poorly managed properties. "When the cat's away, the mice will play" applies to property management. If the property manager knows that the owner will rarely visit the property, that property will suffer the consequences.

How to Oversee Your Property

So how are you doing as an owner overseeing those who manage your property? Do you think there's room for improvement? Here are some suggestions for becoming a more pro-active property owner:

> ➢ Inspect the property regularly, preferably without letting the on-site manager know that you are coming. When you get there, ask yourself:
> - How presentable is the staff? Do they look professional?
> - How is the curb appeal? Is the landscaping well maintained with minimal garbage strewn about?
> - Is there any obvious deferred maintenance?
> ➢ Review the property's operating statements.

- Ask questions. Be curious. If an expense seems particularly high, ask why.
- Review the rent roll. Ask when the last time rents were raised. See if any units have rents significantly below market. If there are, ask why.

Of the three levels of property management oversight, the inspection by the owner is the critical linchpin to successful property management. It is the owner who keeps the on-site manager and the off-site property management company on their toes. Truly, you get what you inspect, not what you expect. How well the owner oversees those who manage their property will in large part determine how well the property performs. With the proactive involvement of the owner, the performance of the property is optimized.

LOAN COVENANTS: AN EARLY WARNING SYSTEM THAT CAN SAVE YOUR PROPERTY FROM DEFAULT

One of the more subtle, but certainly not benign, consequences of the 2008 financial crisis was the decision by lenders to start including loan covenants in their loan documents. Prior to 2008, lenders seldom included any restrictive financial covenants into their real estate loan documents.

What Is a Loan Covenant?

A loan covenant is a condition that the borrower is either required to do (for example, maintain a certain financial ratio) or is forbidden to do (such as add additional debt on the property without prior lender approval). Breach of a covenant can result in a default on the loan being declared, penalties being applied, or the loan being called. In other words, the borrower can have his loan called even if he has never missed a single payment. These loan covenants are often included in the boilerplate sections of the loan documents and are not typically given the attention they deserve.

Anecdotal evidence suggests that business banks are more inclined to have loan covenants in their loan documents than most other lenders. But other types of lending institutions have added loan covenants into their documents in recent years as well.

There are many types of loan covenants, but two of the more common ones are:

1. **Maintaining a minimum debt coverage ratio on the property.** Banks typically require borrowers to generate cash flow from the property of at least 125 percent of the mortgage payment.
2. **Maintaining a specified loan-to-value ratio.** For example, if the value of the property drops so that the loan-to-value (LTV) ratio exceeds 75 percent of the property value, the borrower may be required to pay down the loan to get this ratio in line with the maximum LTV requirement.

Borrowers commonly make three mistakes regarding loan covenants:

1. **Failure to negotiate** – Not all loan covenants are cast in stone. Get a copy of the loan documents early in the process and see what, if any, loan covenants show up in them. Lenders can show flexibility, but you need to begin the negotiating process weeks before loan closing when you have the most leverage to get their cooperation.
2. **Failure to understand** – It is important that borrowers take the time to clearly understand their loan covenants, how they will be monitored, and what will happen if they are not in compliance.
3. **Failure to self-monitor** – Borrowers should monitor their covenants regularly to make sure they are in compliance.

What happens if you find your property out of compliance? Instinctively, we all would like to hide noncompliance from the lender, but the best thing is to take the opposite approach. At the first sign of trouble, the owner should give the lender a full account of what's happening and how the issue will be addressed. Most lenders will appreciate your forthrightness and will try to be flexible. In reality, most lenders are not anxious to add to their portfolio of foreclosed properties, so if they can work with you, they will make every attempt to do so.

Burdensome Requirement or Early Warning System?

I would be the first to agree that loan covenants can be burdensome on the borrower, especially if the loan servicing department shows little desire to work with the property owner. However, loan covenants can also be the property owner's best friend by acting as an early warning system that something is not right with their property or with their personal finances. Having that early warning may give the borrower the needed time to make the difficult decisions that solve the problem before it festers out of control and ends with the lender calling in the loan.

COST SEGREGATION: WHAT IT IS AND HOW IT BENEFITS YOU

Investors often overlook the benefits of completing a cost segregation study on their commercial real estate. Cost segregation is the process of identifying and separating out personal property assets that have been inadvertently combined with a property's real property assets. The primary goal of a cost segregation study is to identify all construction-related costs that can be depreciated over a much shorter timeframe than twenty-seven-and-a-half years for apartments and thirty-nine years for all other property types. Depending on the type of personal property asset, they can be depreciated over five, seven, or fifteen years. As a result of a cost segregation study, property owners can write off their building in the shortest amount of time permissible under existing US tax laws, thus minimizing their overall tax liability.

Here are two important benefits of completing a cost segregation study:

➢ It reduces your taxable income. With accelerated depreciation, you will owe less each year on your federal taxes.

➢ With less taxable income, your property's after-tax cash flow improves, thereby increasing your property's cash-on-cash return.

A cost segregation study will benefit you the most if you meet the following criteria:

➢ Your property costs more than $1 million.

> ➤ You have owned your property for less than ten years.
> ➤ You are in a high tax bracket.
> ➤ You are not planning to sell the property any time soon.

Tax savings vary based on the factors listed above, but as a rule of thumb, every dollar segregated out from a thirty-nine-year depreciated asset to:

> ➤ a five-year depreciated asset is worth 22 cents, and
> ➤ a fifteen-year depreciated asset is worth 8 cents.

For example, let's say you purchased a property for $3,000,000 of which $500,000 was attributable to the land and the balance of $2,500,000 was attributable to the improvements made. After doing a cost segregation study, it was determined that $200,000 of the assets could be depreciated over fifteen years and $100,000 could be depreciated over five years. Based on the rules of thumb shown above, you could expect to save about $38,000 ($200,000 x .08 + $100,000 x 0.22) in income taxes in year one. Understand that this is a ballpark estimate only. But as you can see, the tax savings from a cost segregation study could be considerable.

HAVE YOU FALLEN IN LOVE WITH YOUR PROPERTY?

Over the many years I've been in the commercial real estate business, I've come across all sorts of investors. Occasionally I encounter someone who has fallen in love with his property. Investors such as this approach their property more on how they feel about it than on making sound investment decisions.

Want to find out if you've fallen in love with your property? Answer these questions:

> ➤ Do I consider my real estate a "trophy property"? Do I see it as a real beauty? Do I drive by it and just smile? Do I like to show it off to my friends?
> ➤ Do I make cosmetic improvements to the property for no other reason than I want to?

➢ Would it be difficult for me to sell my property, even at a premium price, because it holds special significance for me? Would it be like selling an old friend? Or has the property been owned by my family for decades and selling it would be tantamount to betraying good ol' Dad?

➢ Do I ignore or am I oblivious to my property's abysmal return on equity because I'm unwilling to refinance the property, even though it's highly likely it's in my best interests to do so?

If you answered yes to two or more of these questions, it's time for an intervention! Yes, my friend, you have fallen in love with your property—but it's not too late to change. Call your team of commercial real estate advisors: your real estate broker, your commercial mortgage broker, your real estate attorney, your property manager, your CPA. Call anyone who will help you see the error of your way. Have them setup an intervention so you can start making real estate investment decisions again based on good and wise counsel.

Sorry for the lame attempt at humor, but I'm trying to make a serious point. Of course, there's no sin in falling in love with your property. There are far worse things you could do, such as neglecting your property altogether or consciously deciding to become a slumlord. But if you decide it's time to manage your property like an investment, here are three suggestions for you to implement to turn things around:

➢ Consider your property an investment, not a love object. As we all know, love can make us do stupid things. Let's limit love to our personal relationships and not to our investments.

➢ Always have a well-maintained property. Have pride of ownership but make improvements that can be justified by either higher rents or an upside in long-term appreciation.

➢ Once a year go through the exercise of determining your property's return on equity (ROE). If it's yielding a return you find acceptable, then leave it alone. If not, take action. Either sell the property or refinance it and pull cash out. The cash back to you from a refinance can be used to purchase another property or enjoyed as you see fit.

RETURN ON EQUITY

I'll cover in the next chapter when it's time to sell a property. Here I'd like to focus on when it's appropriate for an investor to refinance his property. I believe this starts with determining if the property is generating an acceptable return on your money.

What's an acceptable return on your property? For other investment vehicles—stocks, bonds, precious metals, and the like—we have in the back of our minds an acceptable yield we want to achieve. It's not uncommon for my friends to tell me that their IRA or stock portfolio made X percent last year. That's their way of saying that their investments did well (notice they never tell you when they've had a bad year or how much money they lost). It's surprising to me that most real estate investors don't apply the same standard to their commercial real estate investments. So let me show you a simple method I use to calculate a property's return on equity (ROE). To do this, I look at two things:

1. The annual owner distributions. In the example below, to simplify things, we are going to equate owner distributions with cash flow after debt service.
2. The amount of equity in the property, which simply defined is the market value of the property less the mortgage balance.

Let's say that years ago you purchased an apartment for $4 million. At the time of purchase, you financed it with a 75 percent LTV loan or a loan of $3 million with an interest rate of 6 percent. Then a strong rental market significantly increased the property's value to $6 million. In the meantime, you have paid down the mortgage balance to $2 million. Now let's do the math.

Status Quo ROE

Here's how to determine your return on equity if you choose to leave your property's current financing in place:

STATUS QUO

Market Value $6,000,000

Mortgage Balance	– 2,000,000
Equity in the Property	4,000,000
Cash Flow before Debt Service	360,000
Annual Debt Service @ $3M, 6%, 30 Yr Am	– 215,838
Cash Flow after Debt Service	144,162
Return on Equity ($144,162 ÷ $4,000,000)	3.6%

In the status quo example above, the property is currently generating a paltry 3.6 percent return on equity. Would you consider that annual return on your stock portfolio acceptable? Heck no! No way! So why are many CRE investors satisfied with that type of return on their real estate? They shouldn't be.

Refinance ROE

So let's look at what happens to the property's ROE if the property were to be refinanced at 75 percent LTV with an interest rate of 4 percent. Notice it has the same market value and same cash flow before debt service as in the previous example. The only two factors that have changed are the amount of equity in the property and the annual debt service.

REFINANCE

Market Value	$6,000,000
Mortgage Balance	– 4,500,000
Equity in the Property	1,500,000
Cash Flow before Debt Service	360,000
Annual Debt Service @ $4.5M, 4%, 30 Yr Am	– 257,808
Cash Flow after Debt Service	102,192
Return on Equity ($102,192 ÷ $1,500,000)	6.8%

If the owner was to refinance with a 75 percent LTV loan, not only would he increase the property's ROE to 6.8 percent, but he would also get $2,5 million ($4.5 million – $2 million) in cash back! It's a win-win for the investor. He gets a higher ROE on his property and $2.5 million in his pocket to do as he pleases.

Under this scenario, why wouldn't he want to refinance his property? Yet, there are many investors who don't take advantage of refinancing. Are you one of them? Do you have a substantial amount of equity in your properties generating an abysmal return on your equity? If so, it's time to start treating your property like an investment, not as a love object.

Part 4

Selling Commercial Real Estate

15

When Selling Your Property

I made my money by selling too soon.
– Bernard Baruch, businessman, advisor to US presidents

The question all good investors must ask is, when is the right time to sell my rental properties? Is now a good time to divest of my real estate? Before making that decision, here are four questions to ask yourself:

1. What is my time horizon? Am I at a point in life that it may be prudent to invest my money in lower risk investments? Or am I in it for the long haul no matter what?
2. What is my risk tolerance? Can I afford to lose money if the real estate market goes in the tank?
3. Do I need the equity in my real estate for other more important pursuits?
4. How leveraged is my real estate? Or another way to answer that question, where is my property's breakeven vacancy rate? If my property's vacancy rate ballooned to 15 percent or more, would my property still generate a positive cash flow?

How you answer these questions will largely determine the correct course of action for you to follow.

Here are some other reasons that may help you decide if you should unload your rental property.

Good Reasons to Sell

➢ Sell when it's still a seller's market. The best time to dump your property is when the herd is buying. Or at the very least, get rid of it when the real estate market cycle is turning south but well before the herd is aware of it.

➢ Sell when you're running out of viable options to improve the value of your property. If there are no cost-effective capital improvements that will allow you to raise rents, then it might be time to sell.

➢ Sell when you've identified a replacement property for your 1031 exchange that has more upside than the property you currently own.

➢ Sell when interest rates are rising since cap rates will eventually follow. Cap rates are inextricably tied to interest rates. If you believe interest rates will be rising over the long term, then the value of your property will decline over the long term. If you think that is likely, then sell, baby, sell.

➢ Sell when you no longer enjoy owning real estate. If dealing with the day-to-day responsibilities of managing your real estate portfolio is beginning to cause undue stress, that's the time to sell.

Good Reasons Not to Sell

➢ Don't sell just because you see a downturn in the market coming. If you've got a modestly leveraged property that cash flows well and you've locked in a long-term fixed rate loan at a low interest rate, you should be able to successfully hunker down and weather the coming economic storm.

➢ Don't unload your property when everybody else is selling. Fight the urge to follow the herd. Be contrarian. Don't panic. Don't be a lemming. Those who sell when everyone else is selling are the big losers.

➢ Don't divest of your property when future improvements in county or city infrastructure will benefit your property.

➢ Don't sell when the property's neighborhood is in the path of growth. If your property is in a marginal neighborhood, hold on until the path of growth envelopes it. Be patient.

> ➤ Unless you just want to get out of real estate altogether, don't sell until you find a replacement property. Do you really want to pay the capital gains taxes if you don't have to?
> ➤ Don't sell when the real estate market is trending upward. For all intents and purposes, you're leaving money on the table if you do. Be patient.
> ➤ Don't sell if you enjoy owning real estate. Life is good. Don't sell if you don't have to.

I believe that investing in real estate is by far the best way to become wealthy in the United States today. It is certainly better than investing in any other investment vehicle, such as stocks, bonds, annuities, mutual funds, precious metals, and other commodities. But there is a time and season for everything. And the decision of when to sell splits the knowledgeable and experienced investor from those who are not.

FIVE THINGS YOU MUST DO BEFORE YOU LIST YOUR PROPERTY FOR SALE

Let's say, for whatever reason, you've decided it's time to sell your property. There are things you need to do a year or so before you want to sell to get the best possible price for your property. Recall that there are three approaches to valuing real estate:

1. The Cost Approach
2. The Sales Approach
3. The Income Approach

The valuation method the owner has the most control over is the Income Approach. A savvy real estate owner will prepare his property for sale by doing these five things to maximize the property's net operating income.

1. **Raise as many rents to market as possible.** If an owner can raise his most recently signed leases to a higher rental rate than those leases signed three to six months ago, then he has a case to be made to the buyer that

upon turnover the older leases will be raised to the new, higher rents. So be as aggressive on rent increases as possible to maximize the projected net operating income for the property.

2. **Make *cosmetic* improvements to the property.** There are some repairs and capital improvements that can help improve the overall appearance of the property without costing you a lot of money. Keep the property's landscaping looking tidy and well maintained, pick up trash around the property, enclose the dumpster, and power wash the buildings of dirt and debris. Do those things that will improve the overall appearance but are not costly to do. Don't make major capital improvements, like new roofs or painting the exteriors, that are costly since they generally don't increase the value of the property enough to justify the expense.

3. **Get the occupancy rate to market.** Don't even think about selling until you have three or more consecutive months where the property's occupancy rate is at or above the market. If you seek to sell before this time, it will be a big red flag to buyers that there is something wrong with the property. Their solution, then, will be to lower their offer.

4. **Get operating expenses down to a reasonable level.** There are some operating expenses that you have no control over, such as property taxes, insurance, and utilities. Other operating expenses—payroll, general and administrative expenses, maintenance repairs, and capital improvements—can be monitored closely. If you know you want to sell the property in the next year or two, now is the time to reign in these types of operating expenses to help maximize the property's net operating income.

5. If your property is a multi-tenanted retail, office, or industrial building, *get as many tenants re-leased for multi-year lease terms as possible*. Buyers and lenders do not like a tenant rent roll where most of the tenant leases are either on month-to-month or have a year or less remaining on the lease. They also don't like to see a majority of the leases coming due at the same time. Either scenario involves too much rollover risk. Your best bet is to wait to sell your property after you've signed your largest

tenants to long-term leases of three or more years. The longer the lease terms, the better.

DO YOU TAKE A FULL-PRICE OFFER?

After preparing your investment property for sale, the next step is to choose the real estate broker that you think will do the best job representing you. It may be that you have a real estate broker on your real estate advisory team. If so, your decision is already made. If not, then you need to pick one. I suggest you re-read Chapter 5, "Selecting Your Advisory Team," where I outline the process of choosing your team of advisors.

Once you've chosen your real estate broker, the next step is to determine an asking price for your property. Consult with your advisory team for their opinions, especially your real estate broker. However, the bottom-line is that you will need to make the final decision about price. With that important decision made, you're ready to list your property.

Now let's say that, before too long, an investor makes a full-price offer. You're alternately euphoric about getting a full-price offer and wondering whether your asking price was too low. Should you accept the offer? It sounds like an easy answer, doesn't it? But for several reasons, it may not be.

What Is the Offer Contingent On?

In other words, what items must be satisfied in order for the sale to occur? Some contingencies are quite normal to the sales process. All buyers should request that the sale of the property be contingent upon the buyer getting clear title, that the buyer has a reasonable time period to determine the physical condition of the property and to review the property's historical operating statements, and finally that the buyer has adequate time to get financing. As long as each of these contingencies come with acceptable timeframes, you should accept these contingencies; they are reasonable requests.

But what if the offer is contingent upon the buyer successfully changing the zoning of the property? Or the offer is contingent upon the buyer selling his property? Or the offer is contingent upon the seller leasing another space at the property? Then accepting their offer becomes more problematic. In fact, for all three of these examples, I would reject the full-price offer without hesitation.

But what if an offer is made and the decision to accept isn't so obvious? That takes us to the next questions.

What Is the Buyer's Motivation?

Why should you care about the buyer's motivation? Because it may reveal the probability of whether the buyer will actually close on the transaction. Two examples come to mind:

> ➤ Does the buyer intend to convert your property to a higher and better use? If so, the risk associated with that endeavor is much higher than a buyer who simply wants to own and manage your property in its current use and condition.

> ➤ Did the buyer give you a full-price offer just to get control of your property? This is a tactic used to prevent other buyers, maybe buyers who are more serious about purchasing your property, the chance to put an even better offer on the table. Once he has the property tied up, the buyer then renegotiates the price, supposedly because of what was "found" during the due diligence process. In reality, he intended to lowball his original offer regardless of what was found. This tactic can successfully keep your property off the market for sixty days or longer. By taking it off the market for a period of time, the buyer knows that the seller has to weigh the benefit of closing at a lower price than he wanted against the alternative of turning down the low-ball offer and putting the property back on the market without knowing what another buyer will seriously offer for the property.

What Is the Buyer's Real Estate Experience?

Is the buyer well qualified? Does he have a good track record with owning and managing this property type? Or is he new to real estate investing?

Has the buyer even seen the property yet?

Is he local?

Does he have experience in the local market, providing him a better understanding of the neighborhood than an out-of-state investor who doesn't know the market?

Someone who knows the market has a much higher probability of providing a better offer and a higher probability of closing than an investor who does not.

What Is the Buyer's Financial Strength?

Does he have the net worth, liquid assets, credit score, and annual income that lenders would find more than acceptable? Or is his financial strength questionable?

What Is the Buyer's Source of Funds?

Is the buyer proposing to buy the property with a sizeable down payment, making it easier for him to qualify for a loan? Or is he requesting from the lender an aggressive loan-to-value ratio?

Is the buyer assembling a group of investors to buy the property? If so, how far along is he in the process of finding his LLC members? Does he even have experience putting together investor groups? Or is this his first attempt?

As you can see, a full-price offer may not be the best offer. If you are fortunate to have multiple offers on the table, take the time to understand the buyers' real estate track record, their financial strength, and their ability to close. To make an informed decision about which offer to accept, uncover each buyer's motivation for wanting to buy your property and his source of funds to do so. To do otherwise may result in a long, drawn out due diligence period that ultimately ends with the buyer unable or unwilling to close on the purchase of your property.

THREE TRAPS ON THE PURCHASE AND SALE AGREEMENT TO NEGOTIATE AWAY

In Chapter 7, I exposed four potential traps for the buyer on the Purchase and Sale Agreement (PSA). Now let's look at the PSA from the perspective of the seller. Shown below are three potential issues that sellers should do their best to negotiate away before they sign the PSA.[8]

1. Do Not Allow the Buyer to Use "And/Or Assigns"

The phrase "and/or assigns" is too ambiguous and could result in selling the property to an unknown third party that may be unacceptable to the seller. Instead, specifically cover the assignability in the PSA. One scenario would be to allow the buyer to assign the PSA to a party controlled or owned by the buyer. This would allow the buyer to form a new single asset entity to own the property that is under the buyer's control. And it would disallow the buyer to assign the PSA to a third party that is not under the buyer's control.

2. Earnest Money Strategies

The seller should require cash earnest money, not a promissory note, and make the amount substantial. This assures that the buyer is serious and has good financial resources. The seller should also require additional earnest money for extensions of the due diligence period and make sure the earnest money is as nonrefundable as possible.

3. Phase II Environmental Site Assessment

If a Phase II ESA is needed, the buyer should be required to provide a copy of the report to the seller. The seller should also have the right to determine the scope of the Phase II and the choice of environmental consultant. If allowed by law, the buyer should be required to keep the results of the report confidential.

To achieve an optimal outcome when selling a property, negotiate on those issues that are most important to you prior to signing the Purchase and Sale Agreement.

1031 EXCHANGE: WHAT IT IS AND HOW IT BENEFITS YOU

A discussion on selling real estate would not be complete without a rudimentary introduction to the benefits of a 1031 Exchange. The 1031 Exchange got its name from the Internal Revenue Service tax code Section 1031. Simply put, a 1031 Exchange is a deferral of the capital gains tax on the sale of an investment property when it is exchanged for a like-kind replacement property.

When an investor sells his rental property for more than he paid for it, he owes the IRS the federal capital gains taxes on his economic gain. How much the investor owes is dependent on his taxable income. The good news is that the capital gains tax owed can be deferred if the investor exchanges it into another like-kind replacement property. Deferring the capital gains tax is a huge benefit to investors. No other investment asset—not stocks, bonds, or anything else—has this tax deferral benefit.

What is considered a like-kind exchange? Both the relinquished and exchanged property must be held for investment purposes. Properties not held for investment purposes do not qualify for 1031 Exchange treatment. Properties held for investment can be any property that you acquire and hold for income production (rental activities) or for growth in value (capital appreciation).

For a full tax deferral, the investor must meet two requirements:

➤ **Reinvest all net exchange proceeds.** For example, if an investor has $500,000 in net exchange proceeds from the sale of his relinquished property but only invests $400,000 in his exchange property, he has taxable gain on the amount he keeps. In this example, the investor would have to pay capital gains taxes on $100,000.

➤ **Acquire a property with the same or greater debt.** If an investor's debt on his relinquished property totals $800,000 but he acquires his replacement property with only $750,000 in debt, he is subject to capital gains taxes on the difference—in this case, $50,000.

In addition, the investor must meet two time requirements in order to qualify for a 1031 Exchange:

➤ **45-Day Identification Period** – The investor must identify a potential replacement property by midnight of the forty-fifth day from the date of the sale of the relinquished property.

➤ **180-Day Exchange Period** – The investor must acquire the replacement property by midnight of the one-hundred-and-eightieth day, or the date the investor must file his tax return (including extensions) for the year of the transfer of the relinquished property, whichever is earlier.

There are also identification rules for exchange properties:

➢ **Three Property Rule** – The investor may identify up to three properties of any fair market value.
➢ **200 Percent Rule** – The investor may identify an unlimited number of properties provided the total fair market value of all properties identified does not exceed 200 percent of the fair market value of the relinquished property.
➢ **95 Percent Rule** – If the investor identifies properties in excess of both of the above rules, then the investor must acquire 95 percent of the value of all properties identified.

You now know the basic rules of a 1031 Exchange. Congratulations! You now have enough knowledge on the subject to be dangerous. Please, before you sell your next rental property, seek out a qualified expert on this subject—someone who has years of experience as a 1031 Exchange facilitator.

Part 5

The Road Map to Financial Freedom

16

The First Five Steps to Financial Freedom

A big part of financial freedom is having your heart and mind free from worry about the what-ifs of life.
−Suze Orman, financial advisor, author

Congratulations! You've made it to the end of the book. But we're not quite done. This next step in the process is the most difficult because it's the most foundational.

How do you go about implementing what you've learned?

To make all what I've said practical and fully beneficial, you need to understand that investing in commercial real estate really boils down to making five basic investor decisions. Everything else flows from these five decisions, so you need to make them very carefully.

1st Decision: Do you want to be an active or passive investor?

In other words, do you want to make all of the decisions about the property (the active investor) or do you want to defer the decision making to someone else (the passive investor)? The choice is all yours.

2nd Decision: Under both scenarios—active or passive—you have two choices to make.

If you choose to be an *active* investor:

➢ Do you want to be a solo investor working by yourself? Or,

➢ Do you want to be the decision maker for a group of passive investors who want to pool their money to form a limited liability company to purchase commercial real estate?

On the other hand, if you decide you want to be a *passive* investor, where someone else makes the decisions:

➢ Do you want to seek out a traditional real estate sponsor—someone who is well known for his or her real estate acumen? Or,

➢ Do you want to use the services of an online crowdfunding platform to invest your money with?

If you decide that you really want to be a passive investor, once you choose one of the above options, you're done. You have no more investor decisions to make. Kick back and relax.

3rd Decision: If you decide you want to be an active investor, the next decision is who will be on your real estate advisory team?

You can have as few as one—yourself. Or your team members could include some or all of these professions:

➢ Real estate broker
➢ Commercial mortgage broker/loan officer
➢ Real estate attorney
➢ General contractor/building inspector
➢ Property manager
➢ Accountant

I would strongly encourage you to add advisors in those areas where you have little or no experience.

4th Decision: How will the property be financed?

Chapters 9 through 11 laid out your three options. You can:

> ➤ Go back to an existing lender relationship.
> ➤ Shop the mortgage market on your own.
> ➤ Use the services of a commercial mortgage broker.

You know my preference. I believe a commercial mortgage broker, under most circumstances, will get the best possible loan for your property.

5th and Final Decision: How will the property be managed?

Again, you have three options:

> ➤ You can self-manage the property.
> ➤ Hire an on-site manager who reports to you.
> ➤ Hire a property management company to manage the property for you.

Many times, the decision of who manages the property is decided by the size of the property. A small property can be easily managed by the investor. But as the size of the property grows, it is likely that you'll want to turn over the management of the property to an experienced property management firm.

Decision Making **Matrix**
for Commercial Real Estate Investing

---

question 1

Do you want to be an active or passive investor?

⇩ ⇩

ACTIVE **PASSIVE**

⇩ ⇩

question 2a

What kind of active investor will you be?

question 2b

Who will you invest with?

☐ Solo Investor

☐ LLC Managing Member

Proceed to question #3

☐ Traditional Sponsor

☐ Crowdfunding Source

Sit back and relax! Your major decisions are made.

--- *question 3* ---

Who will be on your real estate advisory team?

- ☐ Real Estate Broker
- ☐ Mortgage Broker/Loan Officer
- ☐ Real Estate Attorney
- ☐ General Contractor/Building Inspector
- ☐ Property Manager
- ☐ Accountant

--- *question 4* ---

How will the property be financed?

1.	2.	3.
Go back to an existing lender relationship	Shop the mortgage market on your own	Use the services of a mortgage broker

--- *question 5* ---

How will the property be managed?

1.	2.	3.
Self Managed	Hire an on-site manager who reports to you	Hire a property management company

Those are the five investor decisions that get the real estate investing process rolling. What you decide will in large part influence all the countless other decisions you will make about investing in real estate.

* * *

I wrote this book to be of service to those who are either getting started or have modest experience in commercial real estate investing. A wise man once said, "Learning without execution is useless." Take what you've learned from this book and use it to build wealth and grow passive income from your rental properties.

I realize too that I've given you a lot of information and advice. But you tackle it the same way you tackle any large project: one small step at a time. As the saying goes, "A journey of a thousand miles begins with a single step." The first five steps to financial freedom begin by answering these five foundational questions about investing in commercial real estate.

If I can be of service to you in the future, especially for your financing needs, please feel free to contact me. Good luck and God bless.

Doug Marshall, CCIM
Marshall Commercial Funding, Inc.
(503) 614-1808
doug@marshallcf.com

Appendices

Answer Key to "How Knowledgeable a CRE Investor Are You?"

HOW COMMERCIAL REAL ESTATE IS VALUED

1. When the capitalization rate goes down, the value of the property does what?

   A. Goes down

   B. Goes up

   C. The capitalization rate has no bearing on value

   D. Not enough information provided to make a determination

   Answer: B

   The estimated value of a property is based on the property's net operating income divided by the appropriate capitalization rate (better known as the cap rate). The formula is as follows:

$$\text{ESTIMATED VALUE} = \frac{\text{Net Operating Income}}{\text{Capitalization Rate}}$$

The higher the cap rate, the lower the value. The lower the cap rate, the higher the value.

Use the following information for the next two questions:
- ➤ $5,000,000 purchase price
- ➤ 70 percent maximum loan-to-value ratio (LTV)
- ➤ 1.25 minimum debt service coverage ratio (DSCR)
- ➤ 4.0 percent interest rate
- ➤ 25-year amortization
- ➤ $325,000 NOI

2. What is the capitalization rate for the property?
  A. 4.8 percent
  B. 5.5 percent
  C. 6.5 percent
  D. 7.1 percent

Answer: C

The cap rate is the ratio between the net operating income (NOI) generated from a property and its current market value. The capitalization rate is calculated as follows:

$$\text{CAPITALIZATION RATE} = \frac{\text{Net Operating Income}}{\text{Estimated Value}} \times 100$$

In this particular case, the cap rate is $325,000 divided by $5,000,000 x 100 = 6.5%

HOW THE LOAN AMOUNT IS CALCULATED

3. Based on the underwriting criteria of a maximum 70 percent LTV and a minimum 1.25 DSCR, what is the maximum loan amount (rounded to the nearest $100,000) the property can achieve?

A. $3,000,000
B. $3,200,000
C. $3,500,000
D. $4,100,000

Answer: C

The loan amount is constrained by the 70 percent maximum LTV requirement, not the minimum 1.25 DCR. Shown below are the calculations:

$5,000,000 x 70% maximum LTV = $3,500,000

$325,000 NOI ÷ 12 months ÷ 1.25 = $18,474 per month mortgage payment

4.0 percent interest rate

25-year amortization

Solve for PV (loan amount) = $4,104,804 rounded to $4,100,000

HOW TO CALCULATE A PROPERTY'S CASH-ON-CASH RETURN

Use the following information to answer the next question:
➤ $5,000,000 purchase price
➤ $3,500,000 loan amount
➤ $325,000 net operating income
➤ $221,691 annual mortgage payments

4. What is this property's cash-on-cash return?

A. 4.2 percent

B. 5.8 percent

C. 6.9 percent

D. 7.1 percent

Answer: C

Cash-on-cash return is the ratio of cash flow after debt service divided by the total amount of cash invested, expressed as a percentage.

$$\textbf{CASH-ON-CASH RETURN} = \frac{\text{Cash Flow After Debt Service}}{\text{Total Cash Invested}} \times 100$$

There are two parts to calculating this answer:

a.   Cash Flow after Debt Service = NOI – Annual Mortgage Payments

Or

$325,000 – $221,691 = $103,309

b.   Total Cash Invested = Purchase Price – Loan Amount

Or

$5,000,000 – $3,500,000 = $1,500,000

Therefore: Cash-on-Cash Return = $103,309 ÷ $1,500,000 x 100 = 6.9%

HOW LEVERAGE AFFECTS A PROPERTY'S CASH-ON-CASH RETURN

5. Lowering the interest rate or lengthening the amortization improves the property's cash-on-cash return because in both examples the mortgage payment is reduced. What does increasing the loan amount do to the property's cash-on-cash return?

A. It increases the cash-on-cash return

B. It decreases the cash-on-cash return

C. It has no impact on the cash-on-cash return

D. Not enough information to make a determination

Answer: D

It depends. For example, if you increase the loan amount from 70 percent to 80 percent on the property described above, your cash-on-cash return would be 7.2 percent compared to 6.9 percent for the property leveraged with 70 percent debt. Here is the calculation:

80% Leverage at 4.0% Interest Rate, 25-Year Amortization

a. Cash Flow after Debt Service = NOI – Annual Mortgage Payments

Or

$325,000 – $253,362 = $71,638

b. Total Cash Invested = Purchase Price – Loan Amount

Or

$5,000,000 – $4,000,000 = $1,000,000

Therefore: Cash-on-Cash Return = $71,638 ÷ $1,000,000 x 100 = 7.2%.

This is an example of positive leverage. The more debt, the higher the cash-on-cash return. If you're priority was to maximize your cash-on-cash return, then you would increase the loan amount as much as the lender would allow you to.

But let's assume that the interest rate was 5.0 percent, not 4.0 percent. In this instance, the cash-on-cash-return would go down from 5.3 percent at 70 percent leverage to 4.4 percent at 80 percent leverage. See the calculations below:

70% Leverage at 5.0% Interest Rate, 25-Year Amortization

a. Cash Flow after Debt Service = NOI – Annual Mortgage Payments

Or

$325,000 - $245,528 = $79,472$

b. Total Cash Invested = Purchase Price – Loan Amount

Or

$5,000,000 - $3,500,000 = $1,500,000$

Therefore: Cash-on-Cash Return = $79,472 \div $1,500,000 x 100 = 5.3%

80% Leverage at 5.0% Interest Rate, 25-Year Amortization

a. Cash Flow after Debt Service = NOI – Annual Mortgage Payments

Or

$325,000 - $280,603 = $44,397$

b. Total Cash Invested = Purchase Price – Loan Amount

Or

$5,000,000 - $4,000,000 = $1,000,000$

Therefore: Cash-on-Cash Return = $44,397 \div $1,000,000 x 100 = 4.4%

This is an example of negative leverage. The more you leverage the property, the lower will be the property's cash-on-cash return.

HOW AMORTIZATION AFFECTS YOUR REAL ESTATE INVESTMENT

6. Which amortization method will pay down the loan the fastest?

A. Interest only

B. 30/360

C. Actual/360

D. Not enough information provided to make a determination

Answer: B

Interest only does not pay the loan down at all. The mortgage payment will be exactly the same for the 30/360 and Actual/360 amortization methods. The 30/360 amortization method assumes each month has thirty days and that there are 360 days in a year. The Actual/360 method pays five more days of interest annually, so less of the mortgage payment is applied to the principal. As a result, the 30/360 method will pay down the loan faster than the other two amortization methods.

7. Which amortization method will have the most positive influence on a property's cash-on-cash return?
   A. Interest only
   B. 30/360
   C. Actual/360
   D. Not enough information provided to make a determination

Answer: A

Interest only has the smallest monthly mortgage payment of the three amortization methods, resulting in the highest cash flow after debt service and the highest cash-on-cash return. Let's calculate the numbers to prove it. Using the set of assumptions in Question 4 above, we know that the property generates a 6.9 percent cash-on-cash return when the loan is amortized over twenty-five years. The cash-on-cash return for interest only is calculated as follows:

70% Leverage at 4.0% Interest Rate, Interest Only

a. Annual Mortgage Payments = $3,500,000 x 4.0% = $140,000
b. Cash Flow after Debt Service = NOI – Annual Mortgage Payments
   Or
   $325,000 – $140,000 = $185,000
c. Total Cash Invested = Purchase Price – Loan Amount
   Or
   $5,000,000 – $3,500,000 = $1,500,000

Therefore: Cash-on-Cash Return for the Interest Only option = $185,000 ÷ $1,500,000 x 100 = 12.3%

The difference between a 6.9 percent cash-on-cash return and a 12.3 percent cash-on-cash return is huge! So when a lender offers two or three years of I/O (what it's called in the vernacular), borrowers should take it if their goal is to maximize their property's cash-on-cash return.

8. Which amortization method will the borrower pay more interest over the life of the loan?
   A. Interest only
   B. 30/360
   C. Actual/360
   D. Not enough information provided to determine

Answer: A

Interest only has the smallest monthly mortgage payment of the three amortization methods, *but* all of the payment is applied to interest and none to paying down the principal. With the other two amortization methods, the mortgage balance is slowly paid down. With each payment, a larger amount of the mortgage payment is applied to principal and less to interest. Since no principal is paid with interest only over time, this approach results in paying more interest than the other two amortization methods.

MINIMUM FINANCIAL REQUIREMENTS
LENDERS REQUIRE OF BORROWERS

9. As a rule of thumb, what is the minimum net worth that a borrower needs to qualify for a loan?
   A. 1 times the loan amount
   B. 2 times the loan amount
   C. 5 times the loan amount
   D. There is no rule of thumb requiring the borrower to have a particular net worth in relation to the loan size

Answer: A

Lenders have different net-worth-to-loan ratios, but typically the borrower's net worth must be equal to or greater than the loan amount.

10. As a rule of thumb, what is the absolute minimum amount of liquid assets a borrower must show on his personal financial statement in order to qualify for a loan?
    A. 6 months of mortgage payments on the property
    B. 9 months of mortgage payments on the property
    C. 10 percent of the loan amount
    D. All of the above

Answer: D

Liquidity requirements vary among lenders. Most require, at a minimum, six to nine months of liquidity shown on the borrower's personal financial statement. This is calculated by dividing the total cash on the borrower's personal financial statement by the proposed monthly debt service for the new loan. Other lenders require as much as 10 percent of the loan amount.

Success Principles to Live By

This book would not be complete without sharing with you the success principles that I attempt to live by every single day. Though the wealth and passive income I have been able to accumulate have made my life rich, nothing brings me greater joy than being able to help others. While my greatest influences in life have come from my parents, I have come to realize that the most important success principle is that it's greater to give than to receive. This is my definition of how to live life to the fullest.

THE BOY AND THE STARFISH

About eight years ago, my wife, Carol, and I had the idea of starting a ministry to the hungry and the lonely. The ministry eventually became known as The Jesus Table where people meet every Tuesday night for a meal and a conversation.

When we started, we really didn't know what we were doing. We learned on the fly. One of the ideas that became a signature part of this ministry was having table hosts at every table. There are many benevolent meal sites throughout the Portland metro area, but what makes The Jesus Table unique is our table hosts. Every week they host the same table, so over time our guests begin developing a relationship with the table host of their choosing. The relationship starts slowly, but as the years go by, a deep friendship develops. You see, our guests come for the meal (which is excellent by the way), but their much deeper need is to know that someone cares for them.

One of the couples Carol and I have gotten to know at The Jesus Table is John and Candace Liebertz. They are both recovering addicts who started Fairhaven Recovery Homes, a ministry to alcoholics and drug addicts who have hit rock bottom and want help turning their lives around. Fairhaven provides transitional housing and the necessary structure for those recovering from the ravages of addiction. John and Candace started with one recovery home about nine years ago, and now they are helping about 140 people live clean and sober. Fairhaven continues to grow because the need is so great.

One of the Fairhaven members who came regularly to The Jesus Table for a meal was Mike (not his real name). When Mike originally came to Fairhaven, he was addicted to methamphetamine. But as the months progressed, he did all the right things to live clean and sober. He proved to be so trustworthy and reliable that John and Candace promoted him to be a mentor over one of the Fairhaven homes. For a couple of years, Mike did well overcoming his addiction. But then one day, he relapsed. Mike's relapse reminds me of the story of the boy and the starfish.

There was a young boy walking along the beach. The night before there had been a violent storm at sea, and the seashore was littered with tens of thousands of starfish. As the warmth of the morning sun heated up the sand, the starfish were doomed to die if they didn't make it back into the water. The boy understood their fate and was tossing them back into the ocean when an old man approached him. He said to the boy, "Don't you realize your task is hopeless?" as the old man looked at all the starfish on the beach.

The boy replied, "Not to this one it isn't," as he tossed another starfish back into the ocean.[9]

When Mike relapsed, I felt the emotional pain of losing a friend to the evil of addiction. It hurt deeply. But the good news is that Mike's relapse was short, and he's back on the road to recovery. Through this event, I learned that I can't help every addicted person. The task is overwhelming, but I can help one person in their addiction. And I chose Mike then, and I keep choosing him. I asked Mike if he would like to get together once a week to share a meal and a conversation one-on-one. Soon two more Fairhaven members joined us each week. We are currently going through the Bible book of Proverbs, which has all sorts of wisdom on how we should live. As important as that is, I believe the real hook for these three men—the reason they keep coming back—is that they realize someone who is normal (their word for describing the non-addicted) cares for them.

There are very few families in this country today that are not adversely affected by the epidemic of drugs and alcohol ravaging our country. If you are one of the fortunate few who doesn't have at least one family member caught in the web of addiction, you have a friend or a coworker who is. You can't help everyone, but you can choose to help someone. Choose your "Mike." That person needs to know that someone—you—truly cares.

THREE LIFE LESSONS LEARNED FROM MY FATHER

Even though my father passed away several years ago, I'm surprised how often I think about him. Something happens during the normal course of my day, and it triggers a flashback of him. It wasn't a conscious decision to think about him, but rather a situation that somehow transported me forty years back in time, hearing my dad say or do something.

My father was a good role model in many ways. He also had his faults. But as time passes, the good memories of him are winning out and the not-so pleasant memories are fading. I hope that's what happens with my two adult children when I'm dead and gone.

Although my dad was a good role model, he was a lousy teacher. I don't ever recall him ever trying to teach me an important life lesson. He just lived what he believed. At the time, I didn't understand the importance of or appreciate what I was witnessing. It was just my dad saying or doing what he always said or did. It was nothing special, or so it seemed. It was just vintage Dad. But the older I get, the more I appreciate the values he lived.

Here are some life lessons I learned from my father. You may find them valuable too.

1. Live Well within Your Means

Growing up, my family lived in a very middle class neighborhood. The neighbor on our left was a grocer, the neighbor on our right owned a gas station, and the neighbor across from us was a high school music teacher.

Although my mom drove new cars, I don't recall Dad driving anything but used pickups. A vacation to us was visiting our relatives, certainly not going to a destination resort. We lived quite modestly.

It wasn't until I was in college that it dawned on me that my parents were financially well off. Over the years there had been hints of my parents' wealth, but I hadn't been able to put the pieces together enough to realize that. This changed when Dad, who owned his own CPA practice, sold his business and retired at the age of fifty. He lived quite comfortably for the next thirty-plus years off the income generated from his investments. Living within his means paid off admirably for him.

2. Treat Everyone Equally

After retiring, my dad spent most of his days working on his tree farms. Having grown up in the rolling farmland of Iowa, he was in awe of the beauty of the forests in the Pacific Northwest. About ten years before he retired, he bought a parcel of logged over timberland and spent his weekends nursing the land back to health. He was comfortable working alongside loggers, foresters, and other blue-collar workers associated with the forest products industry. And they were equally accepting of him as one of their own.

I'm not sure why (it's a question I wish I had asked him), but he was politically well connected in Oregon state politics. I remember back in the sixties that he was a pallbearer at a funeral where a fellow pallbearer was Mark Hatfield, the then governor of Oregon.

Dad never showed preferential treatment to his wealthy friends. Those in a lower socio-economic class were treated no differently than the rich and powerful. He treated everyone with the same friendly, Jimmy Stewart-like manner.

3. Put Together Win-Win Agreements

Dad didn't believe in winning at all costs. He proposed agreements that were fair for both parties, not just for him. He had no problem leaving a little bit on the table if it meant getting the deal done sooner rather than later and with both parties satisfied. Sometimes the person he was negotiating with would attempt to take advantage of his desire to strike a fair deal and would respond back with some unrealistic and unjustified counter offer. You see, not everyone plays by the same set of rules. But for the most part, people intuitively understood that he was proposing an agreement that was fair, and they respected him for that.

Sometimes life's most important lessons are better absorbed, not through formal instruction, but by the consistent actions of a role model over a lifetime.

THREE LIFE LESSONS LEARNED FROM MY MOTHER

My mother, who passed away in 1994, was no June Cleaver (the TV mother of Beaver Cleaver in the series *Leave It to Beaver*). Far from it. My mother had very little maternal instinct, and she was quite scary to my friends as she barely tolerated kids in general. Her motto was "Kids should be seen, not heard." In reality, she was harmless, but my friends didn't know that. I learned a great deal from my mother. Here I'll point out just three of her many lessons.

1. When Confronted by a Bully, Don't Back Down

While in grade school, a kid who was a couple of years older than me began bullying me. I told Mom about it, and she told me to fight back. "Don't take his crap" (her words, not mine). So the next time I went toe to toe with the bully, I fought back. He then left me alone and started picking on someone else.

This lesson has served me well over the years. I have had several bosses and clients who have been bullies. They purposely tried to intimidate not only me but everyone around them. I have learned the best way to approach them is not to back down. I tell them what they need to hear, even if I know they won't like it. What I've found is, whether or not they follow my counsel, they at least grudgingly respect me. The problem with this approach in business is that you don't advance up the corporate ladder this way. There's a reason I'm self-employed—and I'm perfectly fine with it.

2. Life Is Not Fair, so Get over It

"Quit your bellyaching" was a favorite saying of my mother. She was not a nurturer. She was in short supply of sympathy and empathy. Having come through the Great Depression, Mom had firsthand experience with real deprivation, so she easily dismissed the trivial things I whined about.

I remember early on how much more stoic I was than my friends when something went wrong. They would be blubbering, feeling sorry for themselves, and I would be rolling my eyes thinking, *Suck it up*.

In reality, life is not fair. We all know that, but the sooner we come to that realization the sooner we learn to be thankful for those many blessings we do have. The alternative is to become bitter at every slight, real or imagined, that happens to us throughout the day.

3. Diplomacy Is for Sissies

My mom was an excellent judge of character. And although she was often too critical of the faults of others, she really was right on her assessment of the situation or the person. She did not "suffer fools gladly." She had no problem telling people what she was thinking and with little consideration for their feelings. Unfortunately, I'm not much better in this regard. I too am known for being brutally honest with people. I really don't know any other way to be. It would be so much easier if I had the ability to tell those little white lies that smooth over difficult situations, but that's not who I am. How many times in a week do I get a telephone call from a prospect who needs to hear that his property, as it stands now, is not financeable? He has called more people than he can count, but none have told him the truth. Instead, to get him off the phone quickly, they refer him to another lender or commercial mortgage broker, and he eventually ends up calling me, only to hear the honest truth no one else was willing to say.

Mom was flawed in many ways (aren't we all), but in hindsight I am so grateful that she toughened me up to take on life's challenges head on. And if she were alive today, I would sincerely thank her for that.

Although my mom was at times a difficult person to be around, it was obvious she loved her family. She just showed it differently. I learned many important life lessons from her, and for good or ill, she has influenced me much more than my kindhearted, well-liked father.

Do People Trust You?
The Thirteen Behaviors of High-Trust People

Years ago, I was employed as a loan officer at a small bank. I enjoyed working for my immediate boss, but the more I got to know the bank president, the more concerned I became. You see, this man didn't mind cutting ethical corners in small ways, and he demonstrated a complete lack of integrity toward his employees. Have you ever worked for someone you didn't trust?

After about three years with the bank, I realized that I couldn't continue working there because I didn't respect the bank president. Fortunately, I was able to find employment elsewhere since the economy was still going strong.

On the way out the door, I remember saying to my fellow employees that when the next recession occurs, this man won't think twice about laying them off. When the economy collapsed into the Great Recession, my premonition proved true. It wasn't just that he laid people off. In all fairness to the bank president, lots of people in real estate lending were being let go. It wasn't what he did but how he did it. His behavior exhibited a lack of empathy and respect for those who lost their jobs.

Now fast-forward several years. While vacationing on the Oregon coast, I read an insightful book on the topic of trust titled *The Speed of Trust: The One Thing That Changes Everything*, by Stephen M. R. Covey (his father was the author of the *Seven Habits of Highly Effective People*). As I was reading, I couldn't help thinking back about the bank president. You see, he violated several of the principles outlined in the book for generating trust.

How about you? Are you someone people naturally trust? Do you know the behaviors that high-trust people exhibit? In this book, the author identifies thirteen behaviors that build trust between individuals.[10]

Behavior #1: Talk Straight

Be honest. Tell the truth. Let people know where you stand. Use simple language. Call things what they are. Demonstrate integrity. Don't manipulate people or distort facts. Don't spin the truth. Don't leave false impressions.

Behavior #2: Demonstrate Respect

Behave in ways that show fundamental respect for people. Respect the dignity of every person and every role. Treat everyone with respect, especially those who can't do anything for you. Behave in ways that demonstrate caring and concern. Don't fake caring.

Behavior #3: Create Transparency

Tell the truth in a way people can verify. Get real and genuine. Be open and authentic. Err on the side of disclosure. Operate on the premise of "What you see is what you get." Don't have hidden agendas. Don't hide information.

Behavior #4: Right Wrongs

Make things right when you're wrong. Apologize quickly. Make restitution where possible. Demonstrate personal humility. Don't cover things up. Don't let pride get in the way of doing the right thing.

Behavior #5: Show Loyalty

Give credit to others for their part in bringing about favorable results. Speak about people as if they were present. Represent others who aren't there to speak for themselves. Don't bad-mouth others behind their backs. Don't disclose others' private information.

Behavior #6: Deliver Results

Establish a track record of results. Get the right things done. Make things happen. Accomplish what you're hired to do. Be on time and within budget. Don't overpromise and under deliver. Don't make excuses for not delivering.

Behavior #7: Get Better

Continuously improve. Increase your capabilities. Be a constant learner. Develop feedback systems. Act on the feedback you receive. Thank people for feedback. Don't assume today's knowledge and skills will be sufficient for tomorrow's challenges.

Behavior #8: Confront Reality

Take issues head on, even the "undiscussables." Address the tough stuff directly. Acknowledge the unsaid. Don't skirt the real issues. Don't bury your head in the sand.

Behavior #9: Clarify Expectations

Disclose and reveal expectations. Discuss them. Renegotiate them if needed. Don't violate expectations. Don't assume that expectations are clear and shared.

Behavior #10: Practice Accountability

Hold yourself accountable. Hold others accountable. Take responsibility for results. Be clear on how you'll communicate how you're doing—and others are doing. Don't blame others or point fingers when things go wrong.

Behavior #11: Listen First

Listen before you speak. Understand. Diagnose. Don't assume you know what matters most to others. Don't presume you have all the answers—or all the questions.

Behavior #12: Keep Commitments

Say what you're going to do, then do what you say you're going to do. Make commitments carefully and keep them. Don't break confidences. Make keeping commitments the symbol of your honor.

Behavior #13: Extend Trust

Demonstrate a propensity to trust. Extend trust abundantly to those who have earned your trust. Extend trust conditionally to those who are earning your trust. Don't withhold trust because there is risk involved.

When people have confidence in you, in your integrity, and in your abilities to perform as promised, trust is the end result. And when potential clients trust you, your chances of getting their business improves dramatically. On a personal level, high-trust individuals are more likely to be promoted, make more money, and have more fulfilling relationships. So the benefits of trust are huge both personally and professionally.

THREE PRINCIPLES STEVE JOBS LIVED BY

A couple of years ago, I read the excellent biography of Steve Jobs by Walter Isaacson. Titled simply *Steve Jobs*, Isaacson does not sugarcoat Jobs' personality in his book. I think Jobs would have been an awful person to work for since he could either profusely praise his employees or call them a piece of sh**, sometimes on the very same day. To say the least, he was a very difficult person to be around. That said, a hundred years from now I believe he will be remembered as one of the great men of our era, held in the same high esteem as Henry Ford, Alexander Graham Bell, and Thomas Edison.

So what can we learn from Steve Jobs? What made him unique? What made him highly successful? There were many traits that made him succeed, far too many to list here, but I would like to mention three:

1. **He had an absolute passion for his work.** What Jobs did was never about getting rich; it was all about making something he believed in. He passionately believed in the Macintosh computer, the iPod, the iPhone, and the iPad, to name just a few of the products Apple developed. A recent survey indicated that 80 percent of Americans are not passionate about *anything*! What are you passionate about? Are you passionate about your work? Do you find excuses to work late or come in over the weekend because what you do excites you? Or do you even know what passion feels like?

2. **He had an obsessive attention to detail.** There was a book written a while ago titled *Don't Sweat the Small Stuff—and It's All Small Stuff.* Jobs would have heaped scorn on the author of that book, for Jobs was all about the small stuff. Good enough was never good enough for Jobs. He was all about hiring the most gifted people he could find and then working them to their extreme limit. Conversely, he would also not hesitate to ridicule and quickly fire those who did not meet his high standards. He pushed and prodded his talented minions to perform at higher levels than they thought possible, resulting in many technological breakthroughs that Apple is now known for. He was absolutely ruthless on his employees, but afterward they grudgingly loved and worshiped him for it. How often do you settle for results that are less than your very, absolute best?

3. **He was a value creator.** He didn't invent many things outright, but he was a master at putting together ideas, art, and technology in ways that superseded what had come before. Jobs once said, "Picasso had a saying, 'Good artists copy, great artists steal' and we have always been shameless about stealing great ideas." Regardless of what we do for a living, our job boils down to adding value in the form of a product or service for either our boss (if we have one) or our clients who are our ultimate bosses. When we stop adding value, we become expendable. What can you do today to add value to your work so your boss or client unhesitatingly realizes your importance in making them more successful?

I have heard people say, "Well, I'm not Steve Jobs." Or they might insert another celebrity entrepreneur in that statement, like business magnate Richard Branson or CEO and chairman of Tesla, Elon Musk. Deep down what they are saying is that they don't have the courage to try to be exceptional. Being average is certainly not the road to success. It is highly unlikely that we will ever be remotely as successful as Steve Jobs, but that should not stop us from living by the business principles that led to his great success.

SIXTEEN COMMON SENSE PRINCIPLES TO LIVE BY

I was recently looking through my archives of articles that I've written over the years. I came across this one titled "Advice for Those Just Starting Their Careers." After re-reading it, I believe a better title would be "Sixteen Common Sense Principles to Live By" or "How to Succeed in Life."

This advice is for all age groups, not just for those starting their careers. I don't recall where I originally came across these principles, but they are certainly pearls of wisdom I'm happy to pass along to you.

1. Seek out and find someone who will mentor you—someone who sees your potential and is willing to develop that potential.
2. Always be learning. Those who succeed in life are continuously learning.
   - Read every day.
   - Take courses.
   - Listen to audio files.
3. Learn the art of active listening. It is safe to say that you never learned a single thing when you were talking. Your willingness to close your mouth and open your ears, on the other hand, will give you the opportunity to add to your learning.
4. Allow yourself to make mistakes and then learn from them.
5. Remember, life is precious. Don't waste it on unimportant things.

6. Set both personal and professional goals. Here are some steps to goal setting:
   - ➢ Decide exactly what you want to accomplish.
   - ➢ Write it down.
   - ➢ Set a deadline.
   - ➢ Make a list to achieve a goal, with all the specifics.
   - ➢ Organize the list into a plan.
   - ➢ Do something every day to move toward a goal.
7. Balance yourself. Don't focus just on your career. Allow time for things that will enhance your emotional, physical, and spiritual well-being.
8. Never seek a job; rather, seek a career.
9. Be willing to take calculated risks.
10. Determine what you are passionate about and then stick to it. Don't let anything sidetrack you.
11. Have as your goal to be the best you can in your profession.
12. Have a positive mental attitude. Avoid being around people who are negative all the time.
13. Be proactive, not passive, about life. Accept complete responsibility for your circumstances. Don't blame them on others.
14. Persevere. Stick at whatever you do until you succeed. Most people fail because they quit too soon.
15. Honesty is an invaluable character quality. Tell people what they need to hear, not what they want to hear.
16. Be a person of integrity. Integrity is defined as strict adherence to a standard or value of conduct. Integrity is not what we do when it serves us. It is who we are when no one is looking, and it is how we treat people who we cannot benefit from.

THE ONE THING:
THE SURPRISINGLY SIMPLE TRUTH
BEHIND EXTRAORDINARY RESULTS

What's the one thing you could do today that would make everything else easier or unnecessary? That question is the premise behind the book *The ONE Thing: The Surprisingly Simple Truth behind Extraordinary Results,* by Gary Keller and Jay Papasan.

For the past thirty years during the month of January, I've gone through the process of setting goals for the coming year. I know that many of you scoff at goal setting, perhaps thinking that it's a fool's errand. For those of you who fall into this camp, now's the time to stop reading. For the rest of you, I highly recommend you read this book by Keller and Papasan. I've read a lot of books over the years on goal setting, setting priorities, living a disciplined life, and the like. In fact, I believe I could write a creditable book on the topic. So it was with grudging admiration that I realized that the authors of *The ONE Thing* were able to broach the subject with several new insights about the topic. Below are three I want to share with you.[11]

Surprising Insight #1

Success is more about establishing new habits than living a disciplined life. I used to believe the myth that the ability to succeed over the long term requires a marathon of disciplined action. What I came to realize is that success is actually a short race—a sprint fueled by discipline, just long enough for a habit to kick in and take over. You can become successful in whatever is most important to you with far less discipline than you think because success is about focusing on the right thing, not about doing everything.

Once you're focused on what is the ONE Thing you should be doing, it takes on average sixty-six days to acquire a new habit. Give yourself the time to develop the new habit. Super successful people aren't superhuman. They've just used selected discipline to develop a few significant habits—one habit at a time.

Surprising Insight #2

Willpower is not always on will-call. It also has a limited battery life. I was under the impression that willpower—namely, the inner strength to control one's behavior—can be called upon at any time of the day. That's another big myth. My supply of willpower is not endless. On the contrary. Willpower is actually in limited supply and must be managed as such. Studies indicate that willpower is a mental muscle that doesn't bounce back quickly. When our willpower runs out, we all revert to our default settings (our bad habits).

So how do you put willpower to work for you? When your willpower is at its highest, you do what matters most. Do your most important work—your ONE Thing—early, before your willpower is drawn down.

Surprising Insight #3

A balanced life is a lie. Balance doesn't exist.

Purpose, meaning, and significance are what make a successful life. Seek them out and you will most certainly live your life out of balance. Extraordinary results require focused attention and time. Time on the ONE Thing means time away from another. This makes balance impossible.

So if achieving balance is a lie, then what do we do? Counterbalance. Counterbalancing is recognizing that you've spent an inordinate amount of time and energy on your life's purpose and that other areas of your life, such as family and friends, have suffered for it. In order to have an extraordinary life, it requires intense counterbalancing so those most important to you are not inadvertently sacrificed on the altar of your life's purpose.

PENDING RECESSION?
EIGHT SURVIVAL TIPS FOR THE CRE PROFESSIONAL

I recently came across this article, "8 Tips to Survive an Economic Downturn," which I wrote in the winter of 2009. As you may recall, our economy at that point in time was in a free fall. The banks were on the brink of collapse, the economy was losing seven hundred thousand jobs a month, and real estate transactions had come to a complete halt. No one was buying or selling real estate. The recession was hitting hard. Life looked bleak. My article spoke to the fear we all felt at that time, and hopefully it generated a bit of hope for real estate professionals who didn't know when they would receive their next paycheck. The time-proven principles outlined in this 2009 article may be the key to surviving the next recession, whenever that may happen.

* * *

The economy is spiraling downward. No one knows where this is heading. Not the experts, not those in high office, no one. What's worse: there is very little you can do to minimize the carnage.

Here are some time-proven principles which, if applied, can help us out of this quagmire.

Go Back to the Basics

For those of us in any kind of sales profession, we learned the critical importance of marketing ourselves when we got started. We learned the hard way that our ultimate success was dependent almost solely on how many marketing contacts we made each week.

Now the phone has stopped ringing. What do we do? We go back and do what made us successful in the first place. Marketing has now become more critical than ever.

Stay Absolutely Focused

So-called "important" issues are often distractions from the overall point of focus for this year—to market like there is no tomorrow. To do anything else will be a distraction from the immediate need to get business through the door.

What one thing do you need to do this year that will best help you survive? Identify it, and forget all the distractions.

Determine What Differentiates You from Your Competition

Consider doing a brutally honest self-assessment about your product or service. What core competency distinguishes you from your competition? Conversely, what do you do that is no different than anyone else?

If you can't differentiate your product or service from that of your competition, you're in deep trouble. You end up being a commodity in the eyes of your clients—just one of many possible choices.

Focus on those things that make you unique.

Be 110 Percent Committed to Your Career

I had a friend, years ago, who was in the same startup struggle I was. I remember him saying that if this did not work out, he had another lucrative opportunity with a newly established dot-com company. I told him I had no other plans. My choice was to succeed as a commercial mortgage broker or fail miserably and utterly. There was no other alternative.

Because I knew the consequences of failure, I eventually succeeded. It was a difficult struggle and took years for me to be successful, but giving up was not an option for me.

It is very difficult to succeed in any profession or any endeavor if you are not 100 percent committed to it.

If Necessary, Redefine Yourself

Sometimes after you go through the self-assessment process, you realize you're not the problem, the market is. If that is true for you, redefine yourself by finding a new market niche within your profession.

For example, a friend of mine works in the residential real estate market, which has been devastated by this slowdown. But he's surviving, having moved much of his business into the reverse mortgage industry, currently a lucrative market.

With every change in the economy, there are winners and losers. Find those clients who are in the most financial pain resulting from the poor economy. They are the ones in need of assistance, and they are motivated to make changes in their current situations.

Stay Positive!

Having a positive attitude, to me, is by far the single most important thing to focus on during difficult times. Here are some suggestions:

➢ Avoid negative people. We all know who they are. Avoid them at all costs.

➢ Quit watching the news. Yes, a lot of bad things are happening right now. But how much of what we hear is overstated or incorrectly stated by the news media in order to create headlines and increase their own market share.

➢ Don't go it alone. Find someone, or maybe more than one person, with whom you can share your deepest fears. Don't be a Lone Ranger.

Deep-Six What Doesn't Work

Albert Einstein once said, "The definition of insanity is doing the same thing over and over again expecting different results." Have you been doing the same thing over and over again expecting different results? A bad economic downturn can sometimes be a blessing in disguise. It can force you to make decisions that you've known in the back of your mind had to be made.

Don't Give Up

In his book *Good to Great*, Jim Collins refers to the Stockdale Paradox, named after Vice Admiral James Stockdale. While in a North Vietnamese prison, he encouraged his men to retain their absolute faith that they would prevail in the end regardless of their difficulties *and* at the same time to confront the most brutal facts of their current reality.

Retain absolute faith that you can and will prevail in the end, regardless of the difficulties you face. At the same time, confront the most brutal facts of your current reality, whatever they might be.

When all else fails, that attitude can carry one through many, many difficult times. Don't give up, no matter what.

* * *

This has, of course, been a recounting of my personal journey. Some of these concepts are mine while many others are not. But then all of us stand on the shoulders of someone.

The Twelve Best Business Books of All Time

I am an avid reader who particularly enjoys reading informative business books. I believe the only way I can stay competitive in my fast-paced business environment is by learning from the masters. Do you have a flaw or area that needs improvement that is preventing you from going to the highest level in your profession? Find a book that addresses your concern.

These authors have compiled incredibly insightful books on a variety of topics. The books are presented in alphabetical order.

Are YOU Ready to Succeed: Unconventional Strategies to Achieving Personal Mastery in Business and Life, by Srikumar Rao

This book is a summary of Dr. Rao's course at Columbia University's Graduate School of Business titled "Creativity and Personal Mastery." The premise of the book is that you are the author of what success means to you. Rao provides many readings and exercises for you to undertake to answer the ultimate question of what brings joy and fulfillment to you personally. The book presents excellent insights in human behavior. Some readers may find this book too touchy-feely, but it is filled with lots of practical applications.

Crucial Conversations: Tools for Talking When Stakes Are High, by Kerry Patterson et al

A crucial conversation is where the stakes are high, opinions vary, and emotions run strong. In other words, all of us on a regular basis have crucial conversations with bosses, business associates, friends, and family. This book shows you how to respond in those critically important conversations so that everyone feels safe to express their opinions and conflict can be resolved amicably.

The E-Myth Revisited: Why Most Small Businesses Don't Work and What to Do about It, by Michael Gerber

There is a fatal assumption that those who go into business typically make. They believe that if they understand the technical work of business, they know how to successfully manage a business. Wrong! This is the reason why 80 percent of all businesses fail in the first five years. To make the leap from working in your business to working on your business is the critical step that most entrepreneurs fail to make. And this is what this book is all about. It is a how-to manual on why you hire others to do the work while you, the owner, focus on the important decisions that can make or break a business.

Getting to Yes: Negotiating Agreement without Giving In, by Roger Fisher and William Ury

This is another excellent book on negotiating agreements. The authors' premise—that any method of negotiation may be fairly judged by whether it meets the legitimate interests of each side and resolves conflicting interests fairly—is durable and takes community interests into account. Some of the chapter titles hint at the methods used for negotiating agreements: "Invent Options for Mutual Gain," "Focus on Interests, Not Positions," "Insist on Using Objective Criteria," and "What If They Use Dirty Tricks." This book is the recognized classic on negotiating agreements.

Good to Great: Why Some Companies Make the Leap and Others Don't, by Jim Collins

Can a good company become a great company, and if so, how? Jim Collins believes any company can become a great company if it conscientiously applies the framework of ideas discussed in his book. Collins identified companies that made the leap from good to great results and sustained those results for at least fifteen years. These companies were then compared to a group of companies that failed to make the leap. The author identifies seven concepts that transformed a good company into a great company.

The Great Game of Business, by Jack Stack

The premise of this book is that the best, most efficient, most profitable way to operate a business is to give everybody in the company a voice in saying how the company is run and most importantly, a stake in the financial outcome, good or bad. This book shows how to develop a financial reporting system so everyone can keep track of the profitability of the company. And if the company does well, the employees receive a financial incentive in the overall success of the company.

The Greatest Salesman in the World, by Og Mandino

Originally written in 1968, this book is a classic on the topic of sales principles told in the format of a parable. Everyone should read this inspiring book.

Love Is the Killer App: How to Win Business and Influence Friends, by Tim Sanders

In the old economy, people could be unsympathetic, mean-spirited, or unkind without any repercussions. Today that behavior can be detrimental to your career. The premise of this book is that those of us who use love as a point of differentiation in business will separate ourselves from our competitors. Love is defined as the selfless promotion of the growth of another. Tim Sanders identifies six reasons why "Bizlove" is the new paradigm in business relationships.

The ONE Thing: The Surprisingly Simple Truth behind Extraordinary Results, by Gary Keller

What's the one thing you can do such that by doing it everything else would be easier or unnecessary? That question and its answer are the focus of this book. And they broach the subject with several new insights. A worthwhile and rewarding read.

Platform: Get Noticed in a Noisy World: A Step-by-Step Guide for Anyone with Something to Say or Sell, by Michael Hyatt

Michael Hyatt is a master at social media marketing. The book is a how-to manual loaded with practical ideas on how to become an influencer in your field, first by blogging and then by using the social media platforms of Twitter, LinkedIn, Facebook, etc. This book is destined to become a classic.

The 7 Habits of Highly Effective People: Powerful Lessons in Personal Change, by Stephen Covey

This book was first published in 1989 and is a recognized classic on self-improvement. Of all the books on a Hall of Fame list of business books, this is the one that has had the most powerful influence on my life. As the title of the book suggests, those who develop these seven habits become successful in business and in life. If you are limited to reading one book, this is the one I would recommend.

The 21 Irrefutable Laws of Leadership: Follow Them and People Will Follow You, by John Maxwell

This is the best book on the topic of leadership that I have ever read. It brings clarity and understanding about leadership while providing step-by-step methods of practical instruction. It is filled with interesting real-life stories that provide support for each of the twenty-one irrefutable laws of leadership.

Appendix 4

Some Essential Sources

During my years learning about real estate and investing in it, I have drawn on a number of resources that have helped me. Here are some of the best I have found, organized according to the chapter content with which they best fit.

Chapter 1   Why Invest in Commercial Real Estate?

"Dividend Yield for Stocks in the S&P 500," IndexArb, February 26, 2014, http://www.indexarb.com/dividendYieldAlphasp.html.

"9 Reasons Why Investing in Real Estate Is Awesome (and Better Than Stocks!)," by Mark Ferguson, *BiggerPockets*, November 10, 2013, https://www.biggerpockets.com/renewsblog/2013/11/10/9-reasons-investing-real-estate-awesome-better-stocks.

"Real Estate Is Better Than Stocks—Fact, Not Opinion," by Ben Leybovich, *BiggerPockets*, November 19, 2013, https://www.biggerpockets.com/renewsblog/2013/11/19/real-estate-better-stocks.

Chapter 2   The Right Time to Invest

"A Bigger Role for Banks in Real Estate Lending," by Mary Ellen Biery, *Forbes*, September 14, 2014, https://www.forbes.com/sites/sageworks/2014/09/14/a-bigger-role-for-banks-in-commercial-real-estate-lending/#6af6786a6ad9.

"The Four Phases of the Real Estate Cycle," by Ian Formingle, *CrowdStreet*, July 15, 2016, https://www.crowdstreet.com/education/article/four-phases-real-estate-cycle.

Chapter 3   Time-Proven Principles of Investing
"Buffett's Annual Letter: What You Can Learn from My Real Estate Investments," by Warren Buffett, *Fortune*, February 24, 2014, http://fortune.com/2014/02/24/buffetts-annual-letter-what-you-can-learn-from-my-real-estate-investments.

"The Seven Immutable Laws of Investing," by James Montier, The Big Picture, March 23, 2011, http://ritholtz.com/2011/03/the-seven-immutable-laws-of-investing.

"7 Million Americans Lost Their Homes during the Recession. Are You Ready to Buy Again?," by Bob Sullivan, April 24, 2015, bob.sullivan.net.

"6 Weekly Habits of Successful Real Estate Investors," by Chris Clothier, *Bigger Pockets*, November 27, 2013, https://www.biggerpockets.com/renewsblog/2013/11/27/weekly-habits-successful-real-estate-investors.

"The World's Most Powerful People, 2016 Ranking–#15 Warren Buffett," *Fortune*, September 2016.

Chapter 4   Do You Want to Be an Active or Passive Investor?
"Top 10 Steps When Reviewing a Passive Real Estate Investment Opportunity," September 9, 2015, astudentoftherealestategame.com.

Chapter 5   Selecting Your Advisory Team
"Investor Mistakes from A to Z," by Dale Osborn, *Bigger Pockets*, http://www.biggerpockets.com/articles/4273-investor-mistakes-from-a-to-z.

Chapter 12   Think Like a Lender to Get the Financing You Want

"From the Analyst Chair: Anticipate the Road Blocks in Commercial Real Estate Finance," by Metropolitan Capital Advisors, blog, September 4, 2012.

"Hook, Line, and Sinker: 12 Examples of the 'Hook' in CRE Finance," by Kevan McCormack, Metropolitan Capital Advisors, April 23, 2013, https://metcapital.com/2013/04/23/cre-finance.

"The Importance of Luck and Timing in Real Estate," by Kevan McCormack, Metropolitan Capital Advisors, August 11, 2012, https://metcapital.com/2012/08/11/financing-commercial-real-estate.

"10 Top Reasons Why Commercial Loans Don't Get Funded," Sofia Capital Ventures, May 13, 2013, http://sofiacapitalventures.com.

Chapter 14   Off-Site Management Decisions to Optimize Your Property's Performance

"Answers to Your Questions about Cost Segregation Compliance," CSSI, http://www.costsegregationservices.com/cost-segregation-compliance-questions.

"Benefits of Cost Segregation," Ernst & Morris, https://costseg.com/wp-content/uploads/2016/10/benefits_corporate.pdf.

"Borrowers Should Negotiate, and Test, Loan Covenants," *Portland Business Journal*, December 6, 2009, https://www.bizjournals.com/portland/stories/2009/12/07/focus3.html.

"Cost Segregation Studies … a Power Tool for Tax Savings," Maxwell, Locke, & Ritter, https://insider.mlrpc.com/resources/special-brochures/cost-segregation-studies.html.

"Cost Segregation Study," *Wikipedia*, https://en.wikipedia.org/wiki/Cost_segregation_study.

"How Can My Loan Be in Default If I Never Missed a Payment?," by Jim Thomas, March 19, 2012, https://www.lexisnexis.com/legalnewsroom/corporate/b/business/archive/2012/03/19/how-can-my-loan-be-in-default-if-i-never-missed-a-payment.aspx?Redirected=true.

"Why Comply? Ignoring Loan Covenants Is a Dire Mistake in Today's Market," by William C. Jenczyk, CCIM Institute, July 2012, https://www.ccim.com/cire-magazine/articles/204430/2012/07/why-comply/?gmSsoPc=1.

Chapter 15   When Selling Your Property

Exeter 1031 Exchange Services, LLC website, http://www.exeter1031.com/article_qualified_use_property.aspx.

"The Power of Strategy: Mastering Advanced 1031 Exchange Concepts," by Scott R. Saunders, http://pdf-book-download.gq/4/9516602/1337759134/992-Power-Of-Strategy-Mastering-Advanced-1031-Exchange.pdf.

"This Is a GOOD Offer—but Is It BEST Offer?," by Allen C. Buchanan, January 20, 2017, http://www.allencbuchanan.com/location-advice/this-is-a-good-offer-but-is-it-best-offer.

Glossary of Commercial Real Estate Terms

The definitions of the real estate terms shown below are meant to give you a quick understanding and should be considered very basic in scope. For more detailed explanations, research these definitions from the multiple sources available online.[12]

1031 EXCHANGE TERMS

1031 Exchange: A deferral of the capital gains tax on the sale of an investment property when it is exchanged for a like-kind replacement property.

Like-Kind Exchange: When both the relinquished and exchanged property must be held for investment purposes. Properties held for investment can be any property that is acquired and held for income production (rental activities) or for growth in value (capital appreciation).

APPRAISAL – THREE APPROACHES TO VALUE

Cost Approach: The cost to build a building similar to the property being appraised.

Sales Comparison Approach: The opinion of value on what similar properties in the vicinity have sold for recently. These properties are adjusted for time, acreage, size, amenities, etc.

Income Approach: Values an income-producing property by dividing the annual net operating income (NOI) by the appropriate capitalization rate.

CROWDFUNDING TERMS

Accredited Investor: Someone who has a net worth of at least $1 million, not including the value of their primary residence, or has income of at least $200,000 annually for the last two years (or if married $300,000 together with their spouse).

Crowdfunding: An internet-facilitated means for sponsors, businesses, or other entities to raise funds from a multitude of individual investors or patrons, even institutions, for a particular project or initiative. For securities-based transactions, the outreach, or open call, is typically limited to accredited investors.

INVESTING TERMS

Cash-on-Cash Return: The ratio of annual cash flow after debt service to the total amount of cash invested, expressed as a percentage.

$$\text{CASH-ON-CASH RETURN} = \frac{\text{Cash Flow After Debt Service}}{\text{Total Cash Invested}} \times 100$$

This financial ratio is often used to evaluate the potential cash flow from income-producing assets.

Internal Rate of Return (IRR): The annualized effective compounded return rate or rate of return that makes the net present value of all cash flows, both positive and negative, from a particular investment equal to zero.

Net Present Value (NPV): A very simple definition of NPV is today's value of all future annual cash flows, both positive and negative, discounted by a discount rate. The discount rate usually represents the desired rate of return on an investor's money.

Return on Equity (ROE): Measures the gain or loss generated on an investment relative to the amount of equity in the property. ROE is usually expressed as a percentage. The return on equity formula is:

$$\text{RETURN ON EQUITY} = \frac{\text{Total Owner Distributions}}{\text{Property Value - Mortgage Balance}} \times 100$$

Return on Investment (ROI): Measures the gain or loss generated on an investment relative to the amount of money originally invested. ROI is usually expressed as a percentage. The return on investment formula is:

$$\text{RETURN ON INVESTMENT} = \frac{\text{Total Owner Distributions}}{\text{Original Investment}} \times 100$$

REAL ESTATE VALUATION TERMS

Capitalization Rate: Better known as the cap rate. This is the ratio between the net operating income generated from a property and its current market value. The cap rate is calculated as follows:

$$\text{CAPITALIZATION RATE} \quad = \quad \frac{\text{Net Operating Income}}{\text{Estimated Value}} \quad \times \quad 100$$

Cap rates are more often used to estimate a property's value. The estimated value of a property is based on the property's net operating income divided by any appropriate cap rate. The formula is shown as follows:

$$\text{ESTIMATED VALUE} \quad = \quad \frac{\text{Net Operating Income}}{\text{Capitalization Rate}}$$

For example, if a property has an NOI of $200,000 and properties of similar property type, size, age, and location have sold recently for a 7.0 percent cap rate, then the property has an estimated value of about $2,900,000 ($200,000 ÷ .07).

Net Operating Income (NOI): The net rental income of a property after operating expenses are deducted. These expenses would include property taxes, insurance, repairs and maintenance, utilities, on- and off-site management costs, general and administrative expenses, etc. NOI does not include the interest expense from the mortgage payment.

UNDERWRITING TERMS–BORROWER

Global Cash Flow: Used in mortgage underwriting to make sure the borrower has sufficient cash flow in order to cover his mortgage payments. Once the borrower's Schedule of Real Estate Owned is completed, the borrower's global cash flow can be determined. It is the sum of all cash flows after debt service of all properties listed on the REO schedule. Some lenders will also include a borrower's personal cash flow on non-real estate assets. This would include sources of income—salaries, social security, and other investment income—less living expenses and debt payments on personal assets, such as auto loans and credit cards.

Global Leverage or Debt Ratio: Used in mortgage underwriting to make sure the borrower is not overleveraged with debt. Once the borrower's Schedule of Real Estate Owned is completed, the borrower's global leverage can be determined. It is the sum of all debt divided by the sum of all the real estate values shown in his real estate portfolio. It is usually shown as a percentage:

$$\text{GLOBAL LEVERAGE} = \frac{\text{Total Mortgages}}{\text{Total Value of All Real Estate}} \times 100$$

The more global leverage a borrower has, the higher the risk to the lender. Generally, lenders would like to see global leverage of no greater than 65 percent.

Liquidity: A person's available cash and marketable securities to pay the mortgage payment. Generally, lenders want to see the liquid assets equal to or greater than six to nine months of mortgage payments on the borrower's personal balance sheet. For example, if the monthly mortgage payment is equal to $10,000, a lender would require $60,000 to $90,000 of liquid assets on the borrower's financial statement.

Net Worth: The value of an individual's assets minus his liabilities.

Net Worth to Loan Ratio: Most lenders require that the borrower's net worth be at least as large as the loan requested. Simply divide the net worth of the borrower by the loan size. During recessions, lenders may require this ratio to be as high as 1.5.

Schedule of Real Estate Owned: A list of all properties owned by a borrower. Typically, an REO schedule includes the property name, address, property type, acquisition date, ownership percentage, lender name, mortgage balance, monthly income, operating expenses, and debt service. From this spreadsheet, the investor's equity and cash flow for each property listed is calculated.

UNDERWRITING TERMS—LOAN

Debt Service Coverage Ratio (DSCR): The ratio of the actual net cash flow divided by the annual debt service:

$$\text{DEBT SERVICE COVERAGE RATIO} = \frac{\text{Actual Net Cash Flow}}{\text{Annual Debt Service}}$$

DSCR measures the ability of a property to meet its regular debt obligations. DSCR is the ratio of the cash flow available for debt repayment to its total debt service. It indicates a margin of safety available should the property rents or cash flows decline temporarily. Lenders usually require a minimum DSCR of 1.20 for apartments and a 1.25 or greater DSCR on all other property types.

Loan to Value (LTV): Expresses the amount of the loan as a percentage of the estimated value of the property. For example, if a borrower borrows $2,000,000 to buy a property with a purchase price of $3,000,000, the LTV ratio is 66.7 percent ($2,000,000 ÷ $3,000,000). The LTV ratio is one of the key factors used by lenders to assess the risk of a borrower defaulting on a loan. Everything being equal, the higher the LTV, the higher the probability of loan default. Lenders generally prefer a maximum LTV of 75 percent on apartments and 65 percent or less for all other property types.

Amortization: The gradual elimination of a mortgage in regular payments over a specified period of time. Such payments must be sufficient to cover both principal and interest. The loan amortization period sets the amount of periodic payments required to pay off a debt obligation. Each payment in the schedule is used to pay interest on the loan and reduce its principal.

Yield Maintenance Prepayment Penalty: Protects the lender against a decline in interest rates. In an environment where interest rates are declining, borrowers typically try to refinance their loans to reduce the interest rate on their debt. If the loan is paid off early at a lower interest rate than when the original loan was closed, the lender loses a high-yielding investment and gets in return a lower rate of return on it. To reduce the effect of an early payoff, lenders often require that the borrower provide compensation, called yield maintenance. The yield maintenance prepayment penalty calculates the net present value of the remaining interest due on the loan to the end of the prepayment period. The loan payoff discount rate would be the difference between the new interest rate and the original mortgage's interest rate. The difference between the two cash flows for the remaining of the balance of the original loan term, discounted to the present, is the yield maintenance prepayment penalty.

MISCELLANEOUS REAL ESTATE TERMS

CC&Rs (Covenants, Conditions & Restrictions): Limit the rules placed on a group of homes by the builder, developer, neighborhood association, or homeowners association. For example, the CC&Rs may prevent an owner from keeping his or her boat or truck on the property.

Commercial Mortgage Broker: Used in contrast with a residential mortgage broker. A residential mortgage broker finances homes. He is unqualified to finance investor-owned properties. A commercial mortgage broker finances investor-owned, income-producing properties. This is an important distinction. And when I occasionally use the term *mortgage broker* in this book, I mean commercial mortgage broker.

Real Estate: Broadly defined as property consisting of land and the buildings on it. My definition has a much narrower scope: Real estate is any investor-owned, income-producing property. Based on my definition, real estate includes single-family rental homes through multi-storied apartments as well as retail, office, industrial, hospitality, mobile home parks, and the like. My definition does not include:

> ➤ Your personal residence as your home since it does not generate cash flow.

> ➤ Undeveloped land as it does not generate cash flow.

> ➤ Owner-occupied properties because the owner is focused on the long-term profitability of his business, not on whether the real estate his business is located on is generating good cash flow.

Cost Segregation: The process of identifying and separating out personal property assets that have been inadvertently combined with a property's real property assets. The primary goal of a cost segregation study is to identify all construction-related costs that can be depreciated over a shorter timeframe, thus owners can write off their buildings in the shortest amount of time permissible, which minimizes their overall tax liability.

Limited Liability Company (LLC): A corporate structure whereby the members of the company cannot be held personally liable for the company's debts or liabilities.

Loan Covenant: A condition of the loan that the borrower is either required to do (e.g., maintain a certain financial ratio) or is forbidden to do (e.g., add additional debt on the property without prior lender approval). Breach of a loan covenant can result in a default on the loan being declared.

Operating Agreement: An agreement among limited liability company members governing the LLC's business and members' financial and managerial rights and duties. Limited liability companies are very flexible in nature, and the operating agreement defines each member or manager's rights, powers, and entitlements.

Notes

1. https://en.wikipedia.org/wiki/CCIM; and "CCIM Secret Sauce: CCIM Education Contributed to Elevating the Entire Commercial Real Estate Profession," by Catherine Simpson Olson, *Commercial Investment Real Estate* magazine, November 2017, 19–22.

2. https://en.wikipedia.org/wiki/Real_estate.

3. The source for all of the facts regarding crowdfunding, except for a few definitions from Wikipedia, come from the Massolution 2015CR-RE Crowdfunding for Real Estate Report. See also "Growth of Real Estate Crowdfunding in 2016," crowdfundingbeat.com, which quotes from the Massolution 2016 Report.

4. Nav Athwal, "Real Estate Crowdfunding: 3 Trends to Watch in 2017," *Forbes*, February 17, 2017.

5. David Drake, "2,000 Global Crowdfunding Sites to Choose from by 2016: Top 5 Growth Indicators," *Huffington Post*, October 22, 2016, www.huffingtonpost.com.

6. The content for the potential traps on the PSA was taken with permission from a presentation by Daniel Drazan, a real estate attorney for Dunn Carney Allen Higgins & Tongue, LLP, August 17, 2016.

7. A special thanks to Jerry Aalfs, Tom Bradley, Tom Fischer and Liz Tilbury who gave valuable input on this section.

8. The content of the potential traps on the PSA was taken with permission from a presentation by Daniel Drazan, a real estate attorney for Dunn Carney Allen Higgins & Tongue, LLP, August 17, 2016.

9. See Peter Straube, *The Starfish Story: One Step towards Changing the World*, eventsforchange.wordpress.com, July 5, 2011, https://eventsforchange.

wordpress.com/2011/06/05/the-starfish-story-one-step-towards-changing-the-world.

10. The following material on the thirteen behaviors is used by permission. For more information on the Speed of Trust, contact Franklin Covey Co., www.franklincovey.com, phone (801) 817-1776.

11. The following insights are drawn from *The ONE Thing: The Surprisingly Simple Truth behind Extraordinary Results*, by Gary Keller and Jay Papasan (Austin: Bard Press, 2013), used by permission.

12. Multiple websites were used to define the real estate terms shown here, including, but not limited to, Wikipedia.com, Investopedia.com, C-loans.com, search.com, Businessdictionary.com, and redfin.com.

About the Author

Doug Marshall is a seasoned commercial real estate professional. For more than thirty-five years, he has worked at mastering the art of commercial real estate investing while securing the best financing possible for his commercial real estate clients. During the last decade, he has also invested in rental properties throughout the Portland, Oregon area.

Doug earned his MBA at the University of Oregon, and in 1999, he received a CCIM designation, which many consider to be the PhD of commercial real estate. In 2003, he founded Marshall Commercial Funding, Inc., a commercial mortgage brokerage firm located in Portland, Oregon.

For thirty-eight years, Doug has been married to Carol. Doug and Carol are the founders of The Jesus Table, a weekly gathering for those in need of a hot meal and friendly conversation. They are also board members of Fairhaven Recovery Homes, a Christian-based ministry that provides transitional housing for alcoholics and drug addicts who are in recovery.

In his spare time, Doug enjoys reading, blogging, golfing, and time in the hammock.

About the Marshall Commercial Funding Website

If you are new to the MCF website (www.marshallcf.com), you may want to access some of the most popular FREE content:

Blog

http://marshallcf.com/blog

The content of this book came from the articles I have written over the years for the readers of the MCF Blog. You can sign up for my newsletter and never miss a new article. Here are three examples of my most popular posts that were not included in the book:

➤ "Fractured Condos: Big Opportunity But Buyer Beware," http://marshallcf.com/fractured-condos-big-opportunity-but-buyer-beware

➤ "A Gathering Storm: 8 Indicators Recession Is Looming," http://marshallcf.com/gathering-storm-8-indicators-recession-looming

➤ "What keeps you up at night? I asked. You answered. See survey results," http://marshallcf.com/2nd-annual-survey-results

---

Mortgage Solutions Blueprint

http://marshallcf.com/mortgage-solution

Here you will find real-life examples of side-by-side comparisons of lender quotes for a specific loan request. Sign up to gain access to these very insightful loan quote comparison spreadsheets.

Glossary of Real Estate Terms

http://marshallcf.com/glossary

To help you better understand the language of the real estate industry, several commonly used terms are provided for your review.

How to Get the Best Possible Loan for Your Property – 10 Part Video Series

http://marshallcf.com/blog-video-courses

Whether you ever do business with us, this ten-part video series provides a step-by-step approach to get the best possible loan for your property.

Property Investing Analysis Spreadsheet

http://marshallcf.com/spread-sheet

This free Excel spreadsheet is a better, more objective approach to valuing a new for-sale listing than you'll find anywhere else. It answers four critically important questions necessary to accurately assess a potential buying opportunity.

Rate Sheet

http://marshallcf.com/rate-sheet

We regularly contact several lenders to determine the most competitive rates in the market. Go to this page and download our rate sheet today.

Recommended Reading List

http://marshallcf.com/book-recommendations

On this page of the Marshall Commercial Funding website are over 240 books divided into twenty-one genres. I heartily recommend each listed resource. Only the best of the best get added to my recommended reading list.

Mastering the Art *of*
Commercial Real Estate Investing

Get exclusive access to Doug Marshall's 35+ years of experience through his private **Question and Answer forum** available only to professionals like you. Each week Doug answers the most pressing questions about CRE investing.

Are you ready to successfully build wealth and grow passive income from your rental properties? Visit: www.marshallcf.com/bonus

---

FREE Bonus Content

You're done reading, but the journey continues! Access bonus online resources at: **www.marshallcf.com/bonus**

Property Investing Analysis template to use for your next purchase. Apply 7 rules of thumb that lenders use to value properties and size loans.

Mortgage Solutions Blueprints archive – real quotes on real deals with actual rates and terms lenders are offering on a variety of property types.

Marshall Commercial Funding Blog – if you liked the book, you'll love getting the twice monthly blog posts sent to your inbox!

To gain access to the Q & A discussion and your free bonus content, go here now: www.marshallcf.com/bonus

The Great Game of Real Estate Investing

Invest like a Seasoned Real Estate Investor

You've read the book, now take a deeper dive into the how-to's of real estate investing. Enroll in Doug Marshall's online course to learn how to master these five critically important concepts:

1 | An Introduction to the Numbers for CRE Investing: Five Real Estate Calculations Every Investor Needs to Know

2 | Develop Your Own Investment Strategy: Five Questions a New Investor Should Answer Before Buying Their First Rental Property

3 | How to Search Out Real Estate Investment Opportunities: The Five-Step Process for Identifying Properties to Purchase

4 | Five Concepts You Need to Know to Get the Best Possible Loan For Your Property

5 | Step-by-Step Instructions for Completing a Property Investing Analysis Spreadsheet

$100 off

Exclusive for readers of this book! Use promo code **BOOK** at checkout.

Marshall Commercial Funding